Doing a Literature Review in Health and Social Care

A practical guide

D0162178

Doing a Literature Review in Health and Social Care

A Practical Guide

Helen Aveyard

 Open University Press

Open University Press
McGraw-Hill Education
McGraw-Hill House
Shoppenhangers Road
Maidenhead
Berkshire
England
SL6 2QL

email: enquiries@openup.co.uk
world wide web: www.openup.co.uk

and Two Penn Plaza, New York, NY 10121-2289, USA

First published 2007, Reprinted 2007,2008 (twice), 2009

A catalogue record of this book is available from the British Library

ISBN-10: 0 335 22261 7 (pb) 0 335 22262 5 (hb)
ISBN-13: 978 0 335 22261 2 (pb) 978 0 335 22262 9 (hb)

Library of Congress Cataloguing-in-Publication Data
CIP data applied for

Typeset by RefineCatch Limited, Bungay, Suffolk
Printed in Great Britain by Bell & Bain Ltd., Glasgow
www.bell-bain.com

Mixed Sources
Product group from well-managed
forests and other controlled sources
www.fsc.org Cert no. TT-COC-002769
© 1996 Forest Stewardship Council
FSC

The *McGraw·Hill* Companies

Contents

Introduction

If you are reading this book, you are probably about to embark on a project or dissertation in which you will undertake a review of the literature. This may be as the dissertation component for your undergraduate or postgraduate degree in nursing, health or social care. This book will guide you through the process of developing a literature review question, searching, appraising and analysing the literature so that you can develop a comprehensive and systematic approach to your review.

A literature review is the comprehensive study and interpretation of literature that relates to a particular topic. More and more students are undertaking a literature review as part of their undergraduate or postgraduate degree for the following reasons. Firstly, research ethics committees and local research governance procedures are increasingly rigorous in their review of student projects and the time taken to prepare a submission for each committee can be many months. This is often a prohibitive factor for many students to undertaking studies involving primary data collection. For pragmatic reasons, many students within nursing, midwifery, social work, occupational therapy and physiotherapy undertake literature-based dissertations instead.

Secondly, literature reviews are becoming more and more important in health and social care. The growing importance of evidence-based practice within health and social care today has led to literature reviews becoming more and more relevant to current practice. In a literature review, all the available evidence on any given topic is retrieved and reviewed so that an overall picture of what is known about the topic is achieved. Thus the method for undertaking a literature review has become an important research methodology in its own right. In this book, literature review methodology is discussed and an approach to undertaking a literature review is outlined, which is suitable for everyone who is new to, or has little experience of, this process.

However, the process of undertaking a literature review is complex and has defined theoretical underpinnings about which you need to be aware if you are undertaking a review of your own. There has been recent discussion of the role of systematic reviews versus the more traditional style of narrative review in undergraduate and postgraduate dissertations. These arguments are debated in journals but are complex and are not in an easily accessible format for novice researchers to engage with. Yet you need to be aware of the arguments and rationale behind both approaches and to be able to justify the approach you take in your review. This book will equip you with the knowledge and skills to do this successfully.

A literature review is also often required as a preliminary introduction to the topic of enquiry that is carried out prior to a primary research study. In this context, the purpose of the literature review is to provide a critical account of the literature in a particular area, in order to demonstrate why a new research study is required. The aim of the researcher is to review and critique the literature relating to the topic of enquiry, in order to demonstrate their understanding of both the research and of the methods previously used to investigate the area. Researchers undertaking a literature review for this purpose must systematically search, critique and combine the literature but their focus is to demonstrate a gap in the existing research base rather than to shed new light on the existing research.

The primary purpose of this book is to explore the literature review as a research methodology for the purposes of developing new insight into a particular area. This book promotes a systematic approach to the literature review process for the novice researcher. It summarises the current debate surrounding the process of undertaking a literature review, including the role of systematic versus narrative style literature reviews, and then gives a clear guide to searching for, critiquing and finally bringing together the literature to form a review. This book is an ideal resource for undergraduate students who are undertaking a dissertation. It is also intended as an introductory text for those studying at postgraduate level or who are new to the process of reviewing the literature. This book will give you a step-by-step guide to undertaking a systematic approach to your literature review.

An overview of the contents is as follows:

- **Chapter 1: Why do a literature review?** To begin, you are introduced to the importance of literature reviews, the different types of literature reviews that exist and what makes a literature review different from other kinds of research and academic writing.

- **Chapter 2: What literature will be relevant to my review?** This chapter gives a clear guide to the many different types of research and other literature that you are likely to encounter when you undertake your literature review.
- **Chapter 3: How do I develop a research question?** This chapter discusses the importance of developing an appropriate research question for your literature review. The research question articulates the purpose of the review and ensures that the review has a specific focus rather than a general discussion of a particular topic. A step-by-step guide to developing your question is given.
- **Chapter 4: How do I search for literature?** In this chapter, the development of a clearly defined search strategy is discussed. The importance of stating clear inclusion and exclusion criteria for the literature you seek is emphasised. This ensures that the search for literature is specifically related to the study question. Irrelevant literature – however interesting – must be discarded, otherwise you will lose track of the focus of the review.
- **Chapter 5: How do I critically appraise the literature?** In this chapter, the process by which you critically appraise the literature is discussed. Appropriate tools for the critique and appraisal of the literature are identified and discussed.
- **Chapter 6: How do I synthesise my findings?** In this chapter, the different methods of comparing and contrasting the literature are discussed. A method suitable for those new to the literature review process is outlined.
- **Chapter 7: How do I discuss my findings and make recommendations?** In this chapter, the writing of appropriate conclusions and recommendations are discussed. It is essential that conclusions and recommendations can be seen to have arisen directly from the results of your literature review, rather than from any preconceived ideas you may have had.
- **Chapter 8: How do I present my literature review?** In this chapter, the importance of appropriate referencing and academic rigour throughout the process of writing a literature review is discussed.
- **Commonly asked questions** Here you will find answers to some of the most commonly asked questions that arise when students are undertaking literature reviews.

At the end of the book, after Chapter 8, you will find a glossary of all the key terms you might need. As you read through the book, you will see these key terms highlighted in the text the first time they are used to indicate that they are included in the glossary. Use this glossary as you read through or for quick reference once you have finished.

1

Why do a literature review in health and social care?

Why are literature reviews important? • Why is there so much available information? • Why does one piece of research often contradict another? • Literature reviews help you to see the full picture • Uncovering new evidence • Encouraging objective thinking • The importance of a systematic approach to the literature review • The systematic review • Less detailed approaches to reviewing the literature • Narrative reviews • The literature review as a research methodology • Can I undertake a literature review for my dissertation? • What is the difference between a dissertation and an essay? • In summary • Key points

It makes sense to begin by defining what a literature review is. In short, a literature review is the comprehensive study and interpretation of literature that relates to a particular topic. When you undertake a literature review, you identify a **research question** then seek to answer this question by searching for and analysing relevant literature. This review leads you to the development of new insights that are only possible when each piece of relevant information is seen in the context of other information.

Why are literature reviews important?

Literature reviews are important because they seek to summarise the literature that is available on any one topic. They make sense of a body of research and present an analysis of the available literature so that the reader does not have to access each individual research report included in the review. This is important because there is an increasing amount of literature available to health and social care professionals, who cannot be expected to read and assimilate all the information on any one topic. Everyone who works within health and social care has a professional duty to be up-to-date with recent developments and ideas that inform their practice. Yet, it is virtually impossible for any one practitioner to assimilate, process and decide how to implement all this information in their professional lives.

Why is there so much available information?

The amount of information available to all health and social care professionals is vast and expands on a daily basis. Every day there are media headlines, reports from conferences, reports of research from scientific journals, expert opinion followed by an opposing expert opinion. There are many reasons for this increase in information available to professionals. It is partly due to the increase in information technology which has led to the increasing availability of information from on-line journals and other websites offering information about health and social care. However, the main reason for the increase in information available within this field stems from the recent emphasis on **evidence-based practice**, which has led to the increasing demand for research evidence upon which practice decisions should be based. Evidence-based practice has been described as a new paradigm within health and social care which has gradually emerged since the 1970s. Practitioners began to question their practice and to search for a scientific rationale for the care they delivered, which previously might have been given according to tradition and experience. As more and more research was carried out and the body of evidence within health and social care expanded, concern about getting this research into practice also increased.

The term evidence-based practice is used to refer to the appropriate application of this research knowledge to practice. Evidence-based practice has been described by David Sackett, founder of the NHS Research and Development Centre for Evidence Based Medicine in Oxford, England, as the 'conscientious, explicit, and judicious use of current best evidence in making decisions about the care of individual patients' (Sackett *et al.* 1996, p. 71).

Evidence-based practice involves identifying a clinical question to answer. One example of a question might be: 'What is the evidence for the use of leeches in wound healing?' The research evidence about leeches in wound healing is then searched for. Are there any clinical trials or is there just anecdotal evidence? The validity or quality of that evidence is assessed and critiqued. Finally, this evidence should be applied to the care of the patient whose need precipitated the clinical question. It is clear that the literature review plays a vital role in promoting evidence-based practice. A comprehensive and competently carried out review enables the practitioner to apply a body of research evidence to practice rather than to rely on – and attempt to interpret – individual studies. This is evidence-based practice in practice!

Why does one piece of research often contradict another?

It often seems to be the case that a piece of research is published one month which contradicts the findings of a piece of research published the month before. For example, one week working mothers are told that preschool care benefits their child and the next they are told that it is better for the child to stay at home. There is often then an outcry – people are confused by the differing messages conveyed and wonder why the results can vary so much. This can be due to the media portrayal of the research in which a complex set of results is reduced to a simplified message. However, it is also due to the fact that any one individual piece of research, or indeed any single piece of health care information, is like just one part of a large jigsaw. It does not represent the whole picture – it represents merely a section of that picture and needs to be set in the context of other information. An individual piece of health care information, taken in isolation, does not necessarily help the reader to achieve a better understanding of the bigger picture towards which the information contributes. There are many reasons for this. For example, the research might have been undertaken in a specific area of practice or with a specific group of people, or sample, and is not generalisable to other areas. Alternatively, there might be flaws in the research design which affect its overall validity. Therefore, when you read a report that seems to conflict with a report you read the previous week and are uncertain as to which report you should consider the most reliable, it is important to consider the merits of each individual report and to remember that each single piece of research contributes just part of the bigger picture and should not be viewed in isolation. This is why literature reviews are so important in health and social care because they enable the reader to view one piece of research within the context of others.

For example, consider the MMR (measles, mumps and rubella) vaccination media stories in 1998–1999. In 1998, Professor Wakefield and colleagues published an article in *The Lancet* suggesting that there was a possibility of a link between the vaccination, autism and bowel disorders. This article was based on a small case study of 12 children who had attended Wakefield's hospital with the aforementioned conditions and who had also had the vaccination. Wakefield stated that there were possible environmental triggers to the development of autism in these children, but without controls this was very uncertain.

It is easy to identify from the basic facts presented in the paper that the evidence conveyed by this paper is not strong. Seen in isolation, this report sparked alarm in both media and medical circles alike. Newspaper headlines led the public to believe that the link between the vaccination and bowel disease and autism to be more certain than Wakefield's report concluded. In addition, there is evidence that many health care professionals felt less confident in recommending the vaccination to parents than they had done before the release of the paper (Petrovic *et al.* 2001). The effect of the adverse publicity surrounding the MMR vaccination which resulted from the publication of this paper is associated with a drastic effect on vaccination rates in the United Kingdom. Prior to the publication of the paper, vaccination rates had been in excess of 90 per cent. Yet Asaria and MacMahon (2006) report that following the publication of Wakefield's paper, as many as 44 per cent of preschool children and 22 per cent of primary school children were unvaccinated in one area of London. As the vaccination rate dropped, the effectiveness of 'herd immunity' was reduced, leading to the reappearance of measles which had previously been almost eradicated. Asaria and MacMahon

(2006) report 449 confirmed cases of measles in the United Kingdom to the end of May 2006 and the first death since 1992. So you can see how important it is to assess critically the value and contribution of any one article before its results are implemented in practice.

Literature reviews help you to see the full picture

The MMR controversy highlights the need to critically scrutinise research reports and this is discussed fully in Chapter 4. The strength of the evidence presented by Wakefield and his colleagues in this early report was not strong. It was based on a sample of just 12 children and did not have a control group. However, it also demonstrates the need for an adequate evidence base which is reviewed and presented in a systematic way, so that an academic judgement can be made about the links postulated by Wakefield rather than a judgement made on one small piece of published information.

This is indeed what happened following the publication of Wakefield's paper. Much research was commissioned in order to explore the possibility of a link between MMR vaccination and autism/bowel disease. Studies were carried out in many countries and gradually more pieces of evidence were added to the jigsaw. Individual studies were published. These were then brought together and systematically reviewed so that the results from each one could be viewed together as a whole (Demicheli *et al.* 2006). As the results from further studies became available and the bigger picture emerged, no evidence was found to confirm the link speculated upon by Wakefield and the fears raised in this early report were not substantiated.

Uncovering new evidence

The MMR controversy provides one clear example as to why it is important to review all the evidence together and how one piece of information can give a misleading picture. Without the comprehensive review of the literature which followed Wakefield's paper, the concerns expressed in his initial paper could not have been refuted. Another example of the importance of systematically reviewing literature is found in the development of the evidence base for the use of the drug streptokinase in the treatment of myocardial infarction, which is now recognised to have saved many lives. Mulrow (1994) discusses how in the 1970s, 33 small clinical trials were undertaken to compare the use of streptokinase versus a placebo (dummy drug) in the treatment of myocardial infarction. These trials were all carried out independently and due to the small size of each trial, most did not find conclusive results in favour of the use of streptokinase. However, these 33 trials were subsequently brought together and reviewed systematically. The results were subjected to a meta-analysis (a process which is discussed in Chapter 5) in which all the results were pooled and reanalysed. The combined results demonstrated clearly the beneficial effect of streptokinase and as a result the drug became part of the standard treatment plan following myocardial infarction, thereby revolutionising care. This review emphasised the importance of reviewing the literature systematically and the limitations of relying on any one piece of evidence. Furthermore, Mulrow (1994) identified that had this review been carried out 20 years earlier, many more lives could have been saved because evidence of effectiveness would have been available earlier.

Encouraging objective thinking

There are other similar examples that illustrate the importance of the evidence provided by literature reviews that are carried out systematically compared to reviews that are not. Take, for example, Linus Pauling, the world accredited scientist, who wrote a book (1986) entitled *How to live longer and feel better*. In this book he quoted from a selection of articles that supported his opinion that vitamin C contains properties that are effective against the common cold. This book makes an interesting and convincing read. However, the arguments presented in the book were challenged some years later by Professor Knipschild (1994), who undertook a systematic review of all of the evidence surrounding the effectiveness of vitamin C and came to very different conclusions. He argued that Pauling had not looked systematically at all the research and had only selected articles that supported his view, while apparently ignoring those that did not. This is why when you read a report by an expert in a particular area, you should remember that his or her report represents just an expert view which might not be substantiated by evidence. This is why expert opinion is generally not considered to be a strong form of evidence.

In summary, literature reviews are important in health and social care because they enable information and research about health and social care to be viewed within its particular context and set amid other similar information and research, so that its impact can be evaluated systematically. Reviewing the literature provides a complete picture, which remains partially hidden when a single piece of research or other information is viewed in isolation.

The importance of a systematic approach to the literature review

The literature review is a vital tool because it provides a synthesis of research and information on a particular topic. It is important that the review is approached in a systematic manner so that all the available information is incorporated into the review. When you read literature reviews, you will discover that some are undertaken in more detail than others. The most detailed type of literature review is often referred to as a **systematic review**.

The systematic review

A **systematic review** strives to identify comprehensively and track down all the available literature on a topic, whilst describing a clear, comprehensive methodology. Systematic reviews have been defined as 'concise summaries of the best available evidence that address sharply defined clinical questions' (Mulrow *et al.* 1997). The most well known method for conducting a systematic review is produced by the Cochrane Collaboration. The Cochrane Collaboration was established in 1993 and is a large international organisation whose purpose is to provide independent systematically-produced reviews about the effectiveness of health care interventions. The Cochrane Collaboration provides detailed guidance about how to undertake the review.

One of the main features of a systematic review is that reviewers follow a *strict protocol* to ensure that the review process undertaken is systematic by using explicit and rigorous methods to identify, critically appraise, and synthesise relevant studies in order to answer a *predefined question*. The reviewers then develop a comprehensive *searching strategy*, and leave no stone unturned in the search for relevant literature, and do not regard the process complete until the search is exhausted. For example, reviewers search for unpublished research and might talk to researchers about unpublished data or articles not accepted for publication, in addition to published data on the topic in question. The reason for this is that there is evidence that a publication bias exists; that results which show clear benefit of an intervention are more likely to be published than those which do not. Thus using only published data could bias the result of the review. Reviewers then develop **inclusion and exclusion criteria** in order to assess which information they retrieve should be incorporated into the review, and to ensure that only those papers that are relevant to the question(s) addressed by the literature review are included. The reviewers then *critique* the selected papers according to predetermined criteria in order to assess the quality or validity of the research identified. Studies that do not meet the inclusion criteria are excluded from the review. This is to ensure that only high quality papers which are relevant to the literature review question are included. The results of research that has been poorly carried out are likely to be less reliable and may bias the findings of the review. Finally, the findings of all the papers that are identified and incorporated for the review are then pulled together and *combined* using a systematic approach. For example, a **meta-analysis** might be undertaken if the results of the research included in the review are reported using statistics, or a **meta-ethnography** can be undertaken if the results of the research included are mainly qualitative. This enables new insights to be drawn from the summary of the papers that was not available before.

The methods of undertaking a systematic review are rigorous and time-consuming. The production of a systematic review usually requires the dedication and effort of a team of experienced researchers over a period of time. Because of the comprehensive nature of the searching strategy, critique and synthesis of the literature, a systematic review undertaken in the detail required by the Cochrane Collaboration is usually considered to be the most detailed and robust form of review that exists. For example, in the United Kingdom they are used in the formulation of guidelines for the National Institute for Health and Clinical Excellence (NICE), whose recommendations for clinical practice are based on the best available evidence. Given the rigorous nature of Cochrane Collaboration systematic reviews, undertaking a review in this amount of detail is beyond the means and timescales of many researchers, especially novice researchers.

Less detailed approaches to reviewing the literature

Even if the stringent requirements of a Cochrane Collaboration style systematic review may not be within the capacity of a novice researcher, it is still possible to undertake a **'systematic approach'** to reviewing the literature. The term systematic review is used by the Cochrane Collaboration to describe the reviews they produce which are carried out according to strict protocol. However, a literature review can be approached in a systematic manner even if the detail required by the Cochrane Collaboration is not attained. While the term systematic review is often used to refer to reviews undertaken according to the Cochrane Collaboration method of reviewing, there is no reason why this term cannot refer to a review of the literature that has been undertaken using a systematic approach, but which is less rigorous and detailed than the methods described above. This means there can be some confusion concerning the meaning of a systematic review. One reader might interpret the term systematic review to mean nothing less than a review conducted using the methods advocated by the Cochrane Collaboration approach, while another reader might accept that a systematic review incorporates a systematic approach but may not reach the same exacting standards.

Undergraduate and postgraduate students who are undertaking a literature review for their dissertation would not normally be expected to achieve a systematic review of the standard required by the Cochrane Collaboration. They would, however, be expected to apply the general principles and guidelines of this approach to produce a literature review that used a systematic approach in the search for, critique and synthesis of the literature. For those new to literature reviewing, it is possible – indeed essential – to achieve a systematic approach to reviewing the literature, otherwise there can be no assurance that the review has been undertaken in a rigorous manner. If a literature review is to be submitted for an academic degree, the method undertaken to review the literature should always be systematic.

Narrative reviews

It is generally accepted that a Cochrane Collaboration systematic review offers the most robust form of evidence for health and social care professionals. However, not all reviews are conducted to this level. Literature reviews vary in the extent to which they are conducted in a systematic manner. For example, a literature review can incorporate a systematic approach but not in the amount of detail as described in the previous section. This approach would be expected of all those submitting a literature review as a component for an academic degree. At the other end of the spectrum there are literature reviews which are undertaken with no defined method or systematic approach. These are often referred to as **narrative reviews**.

Narrative review ----------------------- Systematic review

Undefined methods of searching, critiquing and synthesising the literature   *Explicit rigorous methods of searching, critiquing and synthesising the literature*

There is general concern that narrative reviews do not produce reliable evidence. The lack of a systematic approach to a narrative review is described by Greenhalgh (1997), who makes reference to essays written by medical students who may 'browse through the indexes of books and journals until [they] came across a paragraph that looked relevant and copied it out. If anything did not fit in with the theory [they] were proposing [they] left it out' (p. 672).

The narrative literature review is one that does not use specific identified methods for searching for, critiquing and synthesising the literature. Instead the methods used are undefined and only a small selection of available literature is incorporated in the review, which may or may not have been appraised (Hek *et al.* 2000). There is not a clear indication as to how the review was conducted and therefore the review is not repeatable. Consequently, the conclusions drawn may be inaccurate. These 'traditional' or narrative reviews have a number of biases. There is normally the personal bias of the author(s), a bias in the selection of included material, and with no clear methodology they cannot be reproduced independently, so conclusions cannot be verified easily and may be misleading. The example given earlier about the evidence for the use of vitamin C illustrates this point. Professor Knipschild challenged the findings presented in a narrative style review when he undertook a more systematic approach to a review on the same topic.

The danger of a narrative review: it can lead to misleading conclusions because a comprehensive search for and critique of literature is not undertaken.

In a narrative review, the searching strategy is not clearly defined or organised. There is no specific structure to the searching strategy and it is not clear how the authors search for the literature they identify, how much of the identified literature is incorporated in the review or whether any strategies for critical appraisal of the literature were used. As a result, a narrative review might be no more than a collection of research papers and other information about a given topic.

This may lead to a biased and one-sided review of the literature which is not comprehensive. Individual research papers that are relevant to the review question may be identified but because the search is not systematic, other similar papers may not be identified. The research papers that are identified are then not set in their context but remain like single pieces of a jigsaw. Furthermore, in a narrative review, there is often no clear statement about which studies to include in a review and how these should be critiqued. In a systematic review, predefined inclusion and exclusion criteria are set which determine the relevance of each study identified. In a narrative review, these standards are not defined and any literature might be included without justification or rationale. Therefore, the reader of the review is unclear how much relative importance should be attached to each individual research report included as its merits are not discussed.

While it is acknowledged that a fully systematic approach is beyond the scope of most novice researchers, the narrative review is not a strategy that should be resorted to. Some of the first researchers to raise concern about the quality of the narrative review were Mulrow *et al.* in 1997, who criticised the lack of rigour with which many reviews were carried out. Mulrow *et al.* (1997) examined 50 literature reviews published in four major medical journals and identified that 49 had no statement of the methods used and 47 had inappropriate summaries of the information included. They concluded that, at that time, medical reviews did not routinely use scientific methods to identify, assess and synthesise information.

The main differences between a narrative and a systematic review are summarised below:

- Narrative review
  - no focussed research question
  - no focussed searching strategy
  - no clear method of appraisal or synthesis of literature
  - not easily repeatable.
- Systematic review
  - well focussed research question

- well focussed searching strategy with comprehensive and explicit methods
- rigorous methods of appraisal and synthesis of the literature
- method of undertaking review is explicit and repeatable
- the most detailed reviews require a rigorous and demanding process – not for the faint hearted!

If you are undertaking a review of the literature, you are strongly advised to adopt a systematic approach to the review and to avoid a narrative approach where possible. Those new to reviewing the literature are not normally expected to undertake a systematic review in the detail as required by the Cochrane Collaboration. However, you are required to undertake a systematic approach to the literature review; the possible methods for achieving a systematic approach to a literature review are outlined in the subsequent chapters of this book.

The literature review as a research methodology

It is important to remember that a literature review that is carried out systematically is a **research methodology** in its own right. Your review will have a defined research question and you will follow a systematic approach to answering that question. Even if you are not undertaking a Cochrane-style systematic review, you need to follow a systematic process when you are undertaking your review and you will need to document this process very clearly when you come to write up your review. It is important that you document clearly how you undertook the steps you have taken. The reader needs to know that you undertook a comprehensive and systematic approach to your literature review and the only way to determine this is to give a full account of your literature review process. If you do not document a process that was undertaken, the reader will be given the impression that this process was not undertaken.

There should be a clearly defined section detailing the methods used to address the question. The methods section will usually commence with how you identified your research question. Discuss the rationale for your research question and explore its origins. You can draw on related literature at this point. Remember also to justify your use of a literature review as your chosen research methodology. Why did you not choose another research methodology, such as one involving primary data collection?

You should then document how you searched for appropriate literature. You are advised to include a report of the search terms you used and your search strategy. You should then document how this literature was critiqued and justify your choice of critical appraisal tools. Finally, you need to document how you brought this information together. Present information in a graph or chart if this is appropriate. Overall, your methods section will contribute a large portion of the overall review and is likely to amount to approximately one-fifth to one-quarter of the overall word count.

Finally, your literature review is likely to contain the following components:

- a clearly defined research question
- a clearly documented methods section
- a clear presentation and analysis of the results of your literature search. Relevant literature might include primary research reports, books, discussion articles and other published information. The literature is analysed in order to shed new light on the topic question.
- a final discussion section, in which you make conclusions and give recommendations based on the findings.

Can I undertake a literature review for my dissertation?

Yes. A literature review is particularly suitable for undergraduate or postgraduate students because you can undertake your review from sources that are already published and easily accessible. Undertaking a literature review does not require the formal approval of a research ethics committee, which can be a lengthy process. Students who are undertaking primary data collection (for example, interviews or questionnaires) have to submit a research proposal to their local research ethics committee for approval before they can collect their data. This process seeks to promote the safety of participants who are involved in research. The student who is undertaking a literature review is not required to obtain ethics approval prior to undertaking a review. This is because the reviewer collects data in the form of published material that relates to the research topic and then undertakes to critique and analyse the literature. The reviewer does not have direct access to those who participated in the original research and hence is exempt from seeking the approval of an ethics committee. If you are undertaking a literature review as the **dissertation** component of your degree, this clearly meets the requirements for a dissertation. This book is specifically directed towards students of health and social care who may be undertaking a literature review for the first time when they undertake their dissertation.

While there are many approaches to and types of dissertations, there is widespread agreement that a dissertation should meet the following criteria:

- A dissertation should be an independent and self-directed piece of academic work.
- It should offer detailed and original argument in the exploration of a specific research question.
- It should offer clarity as to how the question is answered.

A literature review meets the above criteria because a review should always commence with a research question which is then addressed in a systematic way. It should be clearly evident that the results of the review arise from the methods used to undertake the study. The aim of a literature review is to uncover new insights on a topic by reviewing the literature in a systematic way. George Watson summarises the essence of a dissertation in his book, *Writing a Thesis*:

> It is not essentially about what is already known; it is about what is unknown or unrealised or misinterpreted. It is concise in its account of familiar materials for just that reason, and expansive only when the crucial point at issue is reached.
>
> (Watson 1987, p. 29)

The student undertaking a literature review moves into the unknown, unrealised or misinterpreted when he or she identifies new insights from the literature that is reviewed. This is not intended to sound like a daunting prospect but rather will be the result of your inquiry. Without the process of bringing together individual pieces of information to complete the jigsaw, an individual research study or other information stands alone and its real impact and relevance cannot be judged. The researcher who completes a literature review is moving from the known (the individual pieces of research and other information) towards the unknown (combining the results of the different information to reach new insights on a topic).

What is the difference between a dissertation and an essay?

Students are often concerned about the differences between an extended **essay** and a **dissertation**. The main difference is that a dissertation always has a focussed research question which is addressed logically as the dissertation progresses. The method with which the question is answered is also addressed.

For example, a dissertation question might be 'What is the role of the social worker in supporting single parents of children under five years of age?' The researcher might then explore the literature to determine what the prescribed roles are and how these roles are played out in practice. The review would be logical, systematic and organised, incorporating all the relevant research and policy concerning the role of the social worker. An essay on the same topic might be entitled 'What is the role of the social worker in supporting single parents'. The essay writer would describe the main body of knowledge surrounding the role of the social worker in this context.

Broadly speaking, the differences between an essay and a dissertation are these:

- The essay title is likely to have a broader scope than the dissertation research question. The dissertation research question is limited to parents of children under five years old. Whereas the essay topic is broader with no such restriction.
- If you are writing an essay, you are expected to summarise the main body of knowledge and information about a particular topic. If you are writing a dissertation, you are expected to develop new insights from the knowledge and information that has been written on the topic.
- If you are writing a dissertation, you are expected to summarise all known information and move towards addressing what is unknown.
- Those writing an essay are not necessarily required to be explicit in the way that they obtained the information to answer the essay question. It is generally sufficient to answer the question without describing the ways in which the information was obtained. Those writing a dissertation are required to give an explicit account of the way in which they searched for, critiqued and brought together all the information.
- If you are writing an essay, you are permitted to refer to key textbooks to answer the essay title. If you are writing a dissertation you are expected to refer back to the original sources wherever possible.

The difference between an essay and a dissertation should be apparent. While an exceptional essay might seek to develop new insights into a particular topic, a dissertation will always aim to do so. Additionally, a dissertation will have a clearly defined research question which is addressed by searching for, critiquing and reviewing the relevant literature in order to shed new light on the topic question.

Characteristics of an essay
- The focus of the topic can be broad.
- A good essay will summarise current knowledge and information on a topic.
- The way in which knowledge is accessed is not necessarily made explicit.
- Textbooks may be referred to rather than original sources.

Characteristics of a dissertation
- The focus of the topic will be well defined.
- A dissertation summarises current knowledge prior to addressing the research question.
- The way in which information is identified is made explicit.
- Original sources are accessed and critically appraised.
- Synthesis of information occurs to offer a new perspective on the topic and to answer the research question.

In summary

You should be starting to see how and why literature reviews are such an essential tool for health and social care professionals. First and foremost, they enable us to gain a comprehensive overview and summary of the available information on a particular topic. Literature reviews are generally more useful to the health and social care practitioner than any one individual piece of research because they allow one piece of research to be viewed within the wider context of others. The process of undertaking a literature review has also been introduced in this chapter. Emphasis has been placed on the importance of the literature review as a research method in its own right and its relevance as a research methodology for an undergraduate or postgraduate dissertation. We have also discussed the need to review the literature using a systematic approach in order to achieve an understanding of the body of literature as a whole in relation to a particular research. As a general rule, when you set out to review the literature, you should aim to undertake a systematic approach as outlined in this chapter, irrespective of whether it is feasible to achieve the detail in the review as required by the Cochrane Collaboration, for example.

Key points

- Literature reviews are an essential tool for those who work in health and social care in order to make sense of the range of information that may be published on any given topic.
- The literature review process is a research methodology in its own right and should commence with a research question, followed by a research design, presentation of results and finally, a discussion of the results.
- The literature review process can and should be approached systematically when undertaken by a novice researcher.

2

What literature will be relevant to my literature review?

Summary of primary research and other sources available • Systematic literature reviews • Quantitative research • Qualitative studies • Analysing qualitative data • Types of qualitative research • The merits of quantitative and qualitative research • Information from other sources • The use of secondary sources • What does the term 'hierarchy of evidence' mean? • Does the 'hierarchy of evidence' apply to my literature review?' • Should I focus my search to empirical/primary research findings? • Why do some literature reviews include predominantly RCTs? • In summary • Key points

You will encounter a large variety of published literature within health and social care that may or may not be relevant to your research question, primarily because there is a vast amount of information that is likely to be available on your topic area. The availability of information on any topic is increasing due to the increased emphasis on evidence-based practice, as discussed in Chapter 1, and the expansion of sources available on the internet. This has the advantage that journals which were previously difficult to access may be available on-line. There is also the potential disadvantage that there is likely to be a proliferation of websites offering information on your topic area, the quality of which will be variable. It's important to remember that not all of the information that you will find will be of good quality and therefore of use to you.

Your first task is to be able to distinguish between the different types of information you encounter and to identify appropriate literature for addressing your review question. Exactly what is relevant to you will depend on your literature review question. Firstly, you need to determine which type of studies and other information are relevant to your review question and to seek out the best kind of evidence to answer this question. This information should be located and incorporated into the review. The second task is to make sense of all the different types of literature you encounter for the purposes of your review. This can be a difficult task for the novice researcher who cannot be expected to be familiar with the many different approaches to research which might have been used to explore the topic area. Furthermore, if you are undertaking a review, you will be expected not only to recognise and understand each research report encountered but also to review and critique it. This is discussed fully in Chapter 5. However, you will often find that one or two research approaches dominate the study of a particular area and it is therefore only necessary to become familiar with a few approaches to research. Despite this, you need to be able to identify the importance and relevance of the literature you encounter. In this section, the different types of literature you are likely to encounter when undertaking your literature review will be outlined.

In the first instance, you will normally be searching for **empirical research/primary studies** or reviews of empirical research. Empirical research/primary studies refer to research studies that have been undertaken according to an accepted scientific method, which involves defining a research question, identifying a method to carry out the study, followed by the presentation of results, and finally a discussion of the results. The term 'empirical' is generally accepted to mean 'based on experience'. An empirical study therefore uses observation, experience or experiment in order to collect new data. Data can be collected in a variety of ways; for example, by questionnaire, interview, direct measurement, observations. Empirical research papers tend to be organised into sections, beginning with a research question, followed by an account of the methods undertaken to address the research question, followed by the results and finally a discussion and conclusion. Empirical research studies are normally the most important types of literature that will be incorporated into a literature review. This is because they attempt to address a specific question using a systematic approach. However, there are also many other different types of literature that will often be relevant in answering your research question. You are likely to consider the other types of **non-empirical evidence**, such as **discussion papers** and expert opinion for inclusion in your literature review. Hek *et al.* (2000) argue that if an area has not been well researched, and there is little research-based information available, then non-research papers, for example, or discussion pieces and expert opinion, can add a wealth of insight into the topic for the reviewer. Important information would be missed if these papers were not incorporated into a literature review as such information adds context and insight, adding depth to the arguments that are already established. An overview of information you are likely to encounter is given in the section below.

Summary of primary research and other sources available

You are likely to encounter a wide range of literature that is relevant to your review question. You need to consider your research question carefully to determine which type of evidence is most useful to you. You are likely to encounter reviews of the literature and reports of original empirical studies, including both quantitative and qualitative research. You are also likely to encounter other information that does not report research findings. These might include discussion papers, consultation papers and letters. Different research questions require different types of evidence. This is discussed in further detail throughout this book. Some examples of published materials that are likely to be encountered are given below:

- **Original empirical research/primary research**
  - Systematic reviews
  - Quantitative research
  - Qualitative research
- **Other sources**
  - Expert opinion
  - Letters
  - Discussion papers
  - Government reports

- NHS policy reports
- Reports from other organisations
- Information from websites
- Patient information leaflets
- Newspapers and magazines

Systematic literature reviews

Systematic literature reviews are referred to as original empirical research as they review primary data, which can be either quantitative or qualitative. As discussed above, systematic reviews which have a detailed research methodology should be regarded as a robust form of evidence when they are identified as relevant to a literature review question.

Quantitative research

Quantitative research, sometimes referred to as positivist research, uses experimental methods and/or methods that involve the use of numbers in the collection of data. Traditionally there is no involvement between the researcher and participant and the researcher stands metaphorically 'behind a glass screen' to conduct his or her research.

For example, quantitative experimental methods have been used to explore whether a lumpectomy is better than a mastectomy in the treatment of breast cancer. Clinical trials were conducted comparing the two treatment options and the results (survival outcomes) were measured numerically in months and years. The researcher divided the participants into two groups, allocated the treatment and observed the outcomes. In principle, quantitative researchers seek causal determination and predictability.

Quantitative research is appropriate only in cases when data can be collected numerically – for example, the number of 'disease-free years' experienced by a patient. Data are analysed using statistical tests. The studies tend to involve many participants and the findings can be applied in other contexts.

Randomised controlled trials

Randomised controlled trials (RCTs) are a form of clinical trial, or scientific procedure used to determine the effectiveness of a treatment or medicine. They are widely considered to be the 'gold standard' for research in which it is desirable to compare one treatment with another (or no treatment). In a randomised controlled trial, participants are allocated by random allocation into two or more groups. To illustrate this most easily, let's say that participants are allocated into just two groups. An intervention is then given to all participants in the first group but not to participants in the second. At the end of the trial, the different outcomes of the participants in the two groups are compared. The researcher is looking for differences between the different treatment groups of the trial that can be attributed to the intervention. It is common for one of the groups to be a control group who receive standard treatment or a placebo group who receive no treatment. A placebo group is, however, only ethical if non-treatment is not thought to be harmful to participants – let's say if there was genuine uncertainty as to the effectiveness of a treatment.

The important feature of an RCT is that the participants are allocated into the different treatment groups of the trial at random. The process of **randomisation** is equivalent to the tossing of a coin. The process ensures that participants are allocated into the different groups by chance rather than by the expressed preference of the patient or researcher. It is very important that neither the participant nor the researcher has any control over the group to which a participant is allocated. This is because the researcher is looking for differences between the different treatment groups of the trial that can be attributed to the intervention. This can only be determined if the different groups, which are commonly referred to as arms, of the trial are essentially equal in all respects except from the treatment given.

For example, if the research participants were to choose which treatment group of the RCT they wanted to enter, it is very likely that one particular treatment group would be more popular than another and the different treatment groups in the trial would not be equal. Let's say that researchers wanted to explore a new drug for helping people to stop smoking. They need to allocate participants by random assignment into one of two treatment/control groups of the trial. If either the researcher or participant had been allowed to choose who should go in each group, those more committed to quitting might have chosen the arm of the trial with the new drug and those who were less committed might have chosen the arm of the trial with the dummy tablet (placebo). The two treatment groups of the trial would then not be equal. It would then not be possible to determine whether the differences in outcomes observed between the different treatment/control groups of the trial were due to the new drug or whether they were due to the differences in the characteristics of the participants who had self-selected into one group or another.

If it is particularly important that participants with specific characteristics are equally represented in both groups (for example, those with young children might have different smoking habits from those without children and you might want an equal number of these participants in each group), then a further form of randomisation can be used called **stratification** (or minimisation) in which a computer-generated process allocates an equal number of people who have or do not have children into each group. This is an additional statistical process that assists in ensuring that the groups are equal in respect of certain predefined criteria that are relevant for the research.

Once each treatment group in the trial has been randomly allocated, the groups are considered to be equal, and the intervention treatment is given to group one. The second group receives either the standard treatment (or no treatment or placebo, depending on the individual study design). The groups are then observed and the differences between the groups in terms of smoking cessation rates are monitored. Given that the two groups of participants were randomly allocated and hence can be considered to be 'equal', any difference in smoking cessation rates between the groups can be attributed to the effect of the drug. A 'null' hypothesis is usually stated when a randomised controlled trial is designed. The null hypothesis states that there is no difference between the two groups. The aim of the RCT is to determine whether the null hypothesis can be confirmed or rejected. If the results show that there is a difference between the control group and the intervention group, then the null hypothesis can be rejected.

A flow diagram of the process of conducting a RCT is presented in Figure 2.1.

RCTs are considered to be one of the best forms of evidence when looking at the effectiveness of treatment. However, if it is not possible to randomise participants in a research study and expose one group to a particular procedure, then it is not possible to carry out an RCT. Thus the randomised controlled trial is one of many approaches to research that will be useful in addressing the research question when undertaking a literature review.

Poster is cited in a smoking cessation clinic for those
interested in entering a smoking cessation trial.

↓

People who respond to the advertisement and fit the inclusion criteria
become the sample. This population is randomly allocated into two groups:

↓

1. Group one receive the new smoking cessation drug.
2. Group two receive standard clinic treatment.

↓

The rate of smoking cessation is compared between the two groups.
Any differences in outcomes is attributed to the different
treatments given that the groups were randomised.

Figure 2.1 The process of conducting an RCT

Cohort and case control studies

Cohort studies and **case control studies** are both observational studies.
These studies attempt to discover links between different factors and are
often undertaken when it is not possible to carry out a randomised controlled trial. They have often been used to find the causes of disease. A
cohort study is the study of a group of people who have all been exposed
to a particular event or lifestyle (for example, let's say that they all
smoke). They are then followed up in order to observe the effect of the
exposure to smoking nicotine on their health and well-being.

For example, one of the most famous cohort studies, which took place
in the 1950s' followed up a group of people and was able to demonstrate
that smoking causes lung cancer. At this time, smoking was considered
normal and harmless and a large percentage of the population smoked.
Many people thought that pollution was the cause of lung cancer. Smoking was not considered to be a risk factor. The epidemiologists the late
Sir Richard Doll and Bradford Hill (1954) conducted a cohort study in
which they followed up a group of doctors, some of whom smoked and
some of whom did not. They then observed this cohort to see whether
those who smoked were more likely to develop lung cancer than those
who did not. This cohort study demonstrated that there was a strong
association between smoking and lung cancer.

A flow diagram of the process of conducting a cohort study is presented in Figure 2.2:

Cohort of people who all experienced the same exposure/experience.

↓

This cohort are followed up to observe the effect of this exposure.

↓

They may be compared to control group who did not experience this exposure, but because the groups were not formed by random allocation, any observed differences between the two groups at the end of the study period is not as easily attributable to the exposure as if the study had been a RCT.

Figure 2.2 The process of conducting a cohort study

A case control study is one in which patients/clients with a particular condition are studied and compared with others who do not have that condition, in order to establish what has caused the condition in the original patients/clients.

For example, Doll and Hill also carried out a case control study examining lung cancer patients and traced back to see what could have caused the disease. They designed a questionnaire which was administered to patients with suspected lung, liver or bowel cancer. Those administering the questionnaire were not aware which of the diseases was suspected in which patients.

It became clear from the questionnaires that those who were later confirmed to have lung cancer were also confirmed smokers. Those who did not have lung cancer did not smoke. Clearly it would not have been possible to have undertaken a randomised controlled trial to explore the causes of lung cancer as it would not have been possible to randomise a group of non-smokers and ask one group to start smoking! It is therefore appropriate to use case control studies and cohort studies to explore relationships between different variables if an RCT is not possible.

A flow diagram of the process of conducting a case control study is presented in Figure 2.3:

Individuals with a specific condition or situation are identified.

↓

The circumstances that led up to the development/progress of this condition are then explored.

Figure 2.3 The process of conducting a case control study

Cross-sectional studies (questionnaires/surveys)

Cross-sectional studies (questionnaire/surveys) are studies in which a sample is taken at any one point in time from a defined population and observed/assessed. A cross-sectional study could be used to assess illicit drug use in a university population, for example. This could be undertaken by the use of a questionnaire or survey, although their use is by no means limited to this research approach. Questionnaires/surveys are printed lists of questions used to find out information from people. They can be used as a means of data collection in randomised controlled trials, cohort and case control studies, and are often used to find out specific information from people at one point in time only. The development of a questionnaire is an arduous process and the information obtained is highly dependent on the quality of the questionnaire developed. There are many potential pitfalls: a long questionnaire might be discarded by the respondent before completion, while complicated or badly worded questions may be misunderstood by the respondent. Postal questionnaires have the additional disadvantage that there is likely to be a low response rate. If large sections of the target population do not respond, the overall quality of data that are collected will be poor. Questionnaires that are administered in a face-to-face interview will generally result in a higher response rate. A thorough exploration of the use of questionnaires in research is given by Oppenheim (1992). In an ideal questionnaire survey, a well designed and piloted questionnaire is administered to an appropriate sample and the response rate is high.

The purpose of a cross-sectional study is to provide a snapshot illustration of the attributes of a given population in the sample, for example, to explore the incidence of illicit drug use at one point in time. The nature of the questions asked can provide descriptive data, for example: 'How many university students use illicit drugs on campus?' Alternatively, some further analysis can be attempted, for example: 'Do all those who report using Class A drugs also report early illicit drug use?'

However, data obtained from a questionnaire study are always limited by the following factors. Firstly, it is often not possible to get access to an entirely representative sample for the distribution of a questionnaire nor is it likely to achieve a complete response rate to the questionnaire/survey. Thus the completed questionnaires will contain information from a selection of, but not a random sample of, students and will therefore give an incomplete picture of illicit drug use. Secondly, any apparent associations arising from the analysis of questionnaire data should be interpreted with caution. For example, if it was identified that those who used illicit drugs also experienced high anxiety levels, it would be tempting to conclude that use of illicit drugs increases student anxiety. However, perhaps the reverse is true and that those with high levels of anxiety resort to illicit drug use. It is very difficult to determine relationships between variables in a questionnaire/survey. For these reasons, cross-sectional studies are not strong evidence for establishing the effectiveness of interventions but are useful for measuring specific actions, attitudes and behaviours of a given group of people.

Qualitative studies

In contrast to quantitative studies, **qualitative research** is concerned with exploring meaning and phenomena in their natural setting. This research is sometimes referred to as naturalistic research. Researchers seek to understand the entirety of an experience. For example, qualitative researchers might explore what it is like for a patient to be diagnosed with breast cancer in order to ensure that adequate support is available to these women. These data are not numerical but are collected, often through interview, using the words and descriptions given by participants. The data are used to generate understanding and insight of the situation being researched. There is no use of statistics in qualitative research, the results are descriptive and interpretative. Some researchers argue that qualitative research is non-generalisable because it is context specific; however, it is now broadly accepted that the insights and interpretations gained from qualitative enquiry are generalisable and can be transferred from one setting to another (Morse 1999).

The fundamental principle of all qualitative approaches is to explore meaning and develop understanding of the research topic. There are a wide variety of approaches to qualitative research. Russell and Gregory (2003) report that over 40 approaches have been identified in the literature. Qualitative data are often collected through the descriptions and words of those participating in the study rather than by numerical measurement as in quantitative research. For this reason, qualitative approaches often use in-depth interviews as the main type of data collection as this allows thorough exploration of the topic with the research participant. Other means of data collection include focus groups and direct observation. The sample, or participants used in a qualitative study, tend not to be selected at random, as is often the case with a quantitative study; instead participants are selected if they have had exposure to or experience of the phenomenon of interest in the particular study. This type of sampling is referred to as **purposive sampling** and this leads to the selection of information rich cases, which can contribute to the answering of the research question. Sample size tends to be small in a qualitative study, due to the need to develop an in-depth understanding of a particular area. This is because researchers are seeking to develop insight into the topic area and a small number of participants who can provide 'information rich' data is more important than a larger sample from whom the data would not be so insightful.

Analysing qualitative data

There are various ways of analysing qualitative data, but most of the approaches involve transcribing recorded interviews, assigning a named code to each section of the transcribed data and then ordering (making sense of) these codes to form categories. These categories are then used to build a description of the results. One of the attributes of qualitative research is that when researchers analyse the data they do not impose their own preconceived ideas onto the data set. They do not set out looking for specific ideas, hoping to confirm pre-existing beliefs. Instead, they code the data according to ideas arising from within it. This process is often referred to as inductive. However, qualitative research is by its nature a subjective enterprise. Researchers do not generally strive to achieve objectivity because this would strip away the context from the topic of research. Furthermore, the researcher cannot achieve complete objectivity because he or she is the data collection tool (for example, the interviewer) and interprets the data that are collected. This is acknowledged in the research process and steps are taken to maintain objectivity as far as possible.

Types of qualitative research

There are many types of qualitative research. Many are described in the literature generically as 'qualitative studies' and are not sub-defined further. However, there are some specific approaches to qualitative research that are further defined. These are outlined below. You need to be able to identify and recognise these different approaches to qualitative research and to understand why one approach was selected for a specific research question.

Grounded theory

Grounded theory was one of the first qualitative research approaches to be documented by the social scientists Glaser and Strauss (1967). The purpose of grounded theory is the systematic development of a theory from a set of data that are collected for the purposes of the research. Data are often collected using interviews and observations. There are specific components of grounded theory that must be incorporated into a study. These are:

- Theoretical sampling, in which the sample is not pre-set but is determined according to the needs of the on-going study.
- Constant comparison analysis, in which data is analysed as it is collected and constantly compared with other transcripts.
- Saturation, in which data collection ceases only when the data analysis process ceases to uncover new insights from the data.

Phenomenology

Phenomenology is the study of the lived experience, or consciousness. Literally, phenomenology is the study of 'phenomena': the appearances of things and the meanings things have in our experience. Therefore, in a phenomenological study, the research topic is studied from the point of view of the lived experience of the research participant. These studies often use in-depth interviews as the means of data collection, as they allow the participant the opportunity to explore and describe the lived experience within an interview setting.

Ethnography

Ethnography is the study of human social phenomena, or culture. An ethnographic study focusses on a community in order to gain insight about how its members behave. Participant observation and/or in-depth interviews may be undertaken to achieve this. Ethnographers typically carry out first-hand observation of daily behaviour (for example, how health care professionals act in a hospital setting) and may even participate in the actual process as a participant observer. Ethnography is fieldwork based and seeks to observe phenomena as it occurs in real time. A true ethnographic study is a time-consuming process.

Action research

Action research or collaborative enquiry, is the process by which practitioners attempt to study their problems scientifically in order to guide, correct, and evaluate their decisions and actions. Action research is often designed and conducted by practitioners who analyse the data to improve their own practice. This research can be done by individuals or by teams of colleagues. The advantage of action research over more traditional approaches to research is that it has the potential to generate genuine and sustained improvements in organisations. These improvements are not imposed on institutions in the form of research findings, but are generated as solutions from within.

The merits of quantitative and qualitative research

There has been much debate in the research literature about the relative merits of both quantitative and qualitative research, with some researchers proclaiming the superiority of one approach over another. In this book, it is argued that these debates are not important. What is important is that the most appropriate research methodology is used to address the research topic in question. There are many similarities between both approaches to research. Both commence with a research question and select the appropriate methodology to answer this question. In all research papers, the methods used to undertake the research should be clearly explained and the results clearly presented.

The research methods outlined above are just some of the methods that you might encounter when you undertake a literature review. It is important that you are familiar with the different approaches to research design so that you can appraise the quality of the literature that is to be incorporated in the review. This is discussed in greater detail in Chapter 5.

Information from other sources

You are likely to come across a vast amount of information that does not report the empirical findings of research, but which is relevant to your research question. Examples of this type of information might include expert opinion, discussion papers, government or health service policy reports and reports from other organisations. Websites will also offer useful information about your topic area. This information can be incorporated in a variety of ways into your literature review; however, the ways in which this information will inform your research question will depend on what your question is. This is discussed further in Chapter 3.

It is important to be aware that the quality of information you may encounter will vary widely. Remember not to believe everything that you read. Remember also that anyone can publish anything on a website, so reliance on information about which you are not sure of the source may discredit your review. It is therefore important to carry out a critical appraisal of all the sources you include in your literature review. This is discussed further in Chapter 5.

Published material relating to your literature review topic that does not report research findings can still be very important to you. Some of this information will be used to set the context for the literature review or to reflect on the findings of the review in the discussion. Sometimes this information might be used to address the research question directly if there is minimal empirical research on the topic. The information might also be used directly to address the research question. For example, if you are looking specifically at how the media portrays the role of the occupational therapist, then media cuttings will be of utmost relevance to your review. However, it is important to consider carefully how you use information that does not report empirical research findings. In principle, when you are writing a literature review, you should be aware that the quality of evidence provided by anecdotal information – even if it is based on expert opinion – is weaker than that which is provided by empirical study.

The use of secondary sources

A **secondary source** is a source that is a step removed from the ideas you are referring to. Secondary sources often comment on primary sources. For example, a report in the *British Medical Journal* (BMJ) might refer to a systematic review published by the Cochrane Collaboration. The BMJ report would be the secondary source and the Cochrane Collaboration report the primary source. You are advised to access the primary source wherever possible and the use of secondary sources should be avoided wherever possible throughout a literature review. This is because if you rely on a secondary report and you do not access the original report, there is a margin for error in the way in which the primary source was reported.

For example, let's say that the author of a paper you are reading (author 1) cites the work of another author (author 2) who has done work in the area. If you refer to the work of author 2 without accessing the original work this is a secondary source and should be avoided when you are undertaking a literature review. This is because in a literature review you are striving for authenticity. Unless you read the original work by author 2 directly, you are relying on another author's report of this work. This means that you cannot comment on the way it is represented by author 1 or upon the strengths and limitations of this work.

It is an important part of the literature review process that you identify the context in which the information is written, so that you are not misled by the way in which the reference is cited. It is easy to see how an author (for example, author 2) can be misquoted in a paper written by author 1. If this paper is then cited by author 3, author 2 can be further misquoted. Ann Bradshaw (2001) provides a good illustration in her historical account of the influences of modern day nursing of how secondary sources have been used to inform influential government reports and how this has led to misleading conclusions. Therefore, where you need to quote an author directly, you are always advised to access this paper rather than to refer to a report of this paper, unless it is not possible to get hold of the primary source, for example if it is out of print or an unpublished doctoral thesis.

What does the term 'hierarchy of evidence' mean?

A variety of hierarchies of evidence have been developed that allow different research methods to be ranked against each other according to the strength of the evidence they provide. There is general consensus that a **hierarchy of evidence** exists and that some forms of research evidence are stronger than others in addressing different types of questions. For example, if you wanted to find out whether glove use was more effective than hand washing in the prevention of the spread of infection, you would find stronger evidence from a randomised controlled trial which looked at a comparison between the two approaches than in a study which asked the opinion of patients or clients as to which method they thought was more effective in preventing the spread of infection. The stronger evidence provided by the RCT in this instance indicates that the RCT should be placed higher up in a hierarchy of evidence than a study exploring patients' perception of hand hygiene when addressing this particular question. In the hierarchy of evidence, the higher up a methodology is ranked, the more robust and close to objective truth it is assumed to be. One of the most well known hierarchies of evidence, which is concerned with ranking the strength of evidence relating to the effectiveness of a treatment or intervention, is that developed by Sackett *et al.* (1996). This hierarchy of evidence goes in this order:

1 Systematic reviews and meta-analyses
2 Randomised controlled trials
3 Cohort studies, case controlled studies
4 Surveys
5 Case reports
6 Qualitative studies
7 Expert opinion
8 Anecdotal opinion

The implication of the hierarchy of evidence for the literature reviewer who has a research question concerned with treatment or intervention effectiveness is that greater weight should be given to relevant research identified that is higher up the hierarchy. For example, for a literature review exploring whether treatment A is better than treatment B, the results of randomised controlled trials would be given more weight than the results of a survey of patients' experience of the drugs, but this would be given more weight than just one anecdotal opinion given by a particular patient or health care professional. However, it is also important to bear in mind that it is not always possible or desirable to undertake an RCT, even if this type of evidence is considered to be required. For example, for researchers looking at infant nutrition, it would not be acceptable to ask one group of mothers to abstain from breastfeeding their babies as a control group for another group of mothers who were asked to breastfeed.

Does the 'hierarchy of evidence' apply to my literature review?'

It is important to note that the particular hierarchy noted above does not apply to all literature review questions. For research questions that are considering things other than the effectiveness of care or treatment intervention, this hierarchy will not apply. In health and social care, knowledge is obtained from a variety of different sources and many different types of research contribute to our understanding of a wide range of situations encountered in everyday practice in health and social care. Research methodologies higher up in the hierarchy will not be the most appropriate way of approaching every research question. It would not be appropriate to denigrate the research methodologies lower down in the hierarchy if they are the most appropriate approach to answering the research question. It is therefore appropriate to say that the most robust form of evidence for addressing a particular research question will be determined *by that research question*. This is discussed further in Chapter 4.

Should I focus my search to empirical/primary research findings?

It has been suggested throughout this book that, dependent on your research question and inclusion and exclusion criteria, primary research articles will normally comprise the main body of your literature review. This is because they are likely to provide the best quality of evidence for addressing your research question. The exception to this is where the research question for a literature review is only answerable through the use of non-research articles. For example, a research question asking how experts perceive the threat from bird flu would clearly incorporate expert opinion as the evidence required to answer the question.

However, most research questions for a literature review are not concerned with seeking expert opinion and, in most literature reviews, the relevant information for addressing the topic area will not be anecdotal evidence. Unless you are particularly interested in analysing the opinions of experts it is important to remember that expert opinion remains opinion only and is therefore not strong evidence. Indeed, some experts might become so engrossed in their subject that they are less able to provide an objective assessment of the topic area (Greenhalgh 1997).

Why do some literature reviews include predominantly RCTs?

Traditionally, the Cochrane Collaboration have always placed great emphasis on the importance of the randomised controlled trial (RCT) in the compilation of a systematic review. This has been due largely to the nature of the questions they sought to address through the reviews undertaken. The Cochrane Collaboration have traditionally sought to address questions about the effectiveness of treatments and interventions; for example, Faggiano *et al.* (2006) published a review which evaluates the effectiveness of school-based interventions in improving knowledge of schoolchildren about illicit drug use. The best evidence to evaluate the effectiveness of an intervention is the randomised controlled trial. The reasons for this are discussed later in this section. However, for literature review questions that *do not* seek to evaluate the effectiveness of a treatment or intervention, randomised controlled trials will not be the best or only evidence to use. There is increasing recognition that randomised controlled trials cannot provide evidence regarding all aspects of health and social care. In many areas of health and social care research, it is not possible to address potential research using randomised controlled trials, or it may be inappropriate to do so. It would not, for example, be ethical to conduct a randomised controlled trial in which one group of participants was randomly assigned to receive large doses of radiation whereas the control group did not. This would cause probable harm to one group of participants. Furthermore, for questions not concerned with effectiveness of treatments or interventions, there are often more appropriate ways of collecting data that will address the research question rather than an RCT. For example, researchers concerned with exploring client experience of day care services would be likely to explore this through interviews with the clients themselves rather than to conduct a trial to explore the differences between two types of interventions. For these reasons, there is increasing recognition that systematic reviews should seek to incorporate the types of research that are most likely to address the research question, rather than limit their inclusion criteria to randomised controlled trials. There is now general acceptance that all types of literature can, and indeed should, be included in a review if it is relevant to the review question.

In summary

You will encounter a wide variety of literature when you undertake your literature review. This is likely to include primary data from quantitative and/or qualitative studies and reviews of these studies, in addition to non-research papers (for example, discussion papers, letters and so on). A summary of this information is included in this chapter to assist you in making sense of the literature you come across. It is important to emphasise that the type of literature you require to address your research is entirely dependent on your research question and you should be guided by this to determine what literature you seek. This is discussed in Chapters 3 and 4. The next chapter examines the importance of selecting an appropriate research question to be addressed in the literature review.

Key points

- You are likely to encounter a wide range of information that is relevant to your research question.
- It is important to identify the types of information that you will need to address your research question.

3

How do I develop a research question?

The importance of a research question

The overall aim for a research question is that, when answered, it should contribute to a better understanding of the practice area considered and ultimately improve patient/client care. You should therefore be able to give a clear rationale for your choice of research question.

Finding the **right research question** is one of the most important aspects of undertaking your literature review. It is very important that you develop a clear research question, as without this, your literature review will not be focussed. Defining a good clear question is often difficult but it is crucial to spend time getting the research question right. If you get the research question right, you will find that you are directed to relevant literature which enables you to answer your question in the most appropriate way. If you get the research question wrong – for example, if your question is vague, undefined or too broad – or indeed if you are not completely sure what question you are asking, you will find that you are unable to focus your study and are led in many different directions to an insurmountable quantity of information which is impossible to process.

The research question provides the **structure** for the whole of the literature review process. A good research question will act as a guide through the process of writing the literature review. It will provide a clear focus and indication as to what type of literature is required to address your question. In contrast, a poor research question will not act as a guide. A poor question will be vague and it will not be clear which literature is most appropriate to address the question. The question is also likely to be too broad and unanswerable within the time frame for the writing of the review. As a result, you are likely to remain unclear about which direction the question is leading you and you are at risk of being led down many paths until you finally discover that you have not actually addressed the question.

An example of a poor question for a small-scale project could be: 'What are the causes of domestic violence?' This is a huge and complex topic on which there is a lot of discussion and research evidence. Within the time span of a small-scale project, the researcher would be unable to cover the breadth of the topic and would be unlikely to be able to reach any conclusion based on the evidence reviewed. This is not to say that the researcher would be unable to comment on the issues surrounding domestic violence, however; it would be unlikely that such a big question could be addressed in a systematic manner. It would not be possible to review all of the available literature and therefore the conclusions drawn would not reflect the full breadth of research and discussion. The components of a good and not so good research question will be returned to later in this chapter.

Given the importance of developing a good research question that is 'do-able' within your time frame, you are advised to get your research question established as soon as you can within the timescale for your review. If your other commitments then demand your time and your literature review is put 'on hold' for some weeks or even months – as is usual for those undertaking their final year of an undergraduate degree – you can return to your review later with a firm idea about what you are intending to do. Indeed, you might find that your approach to the review has developed during the time spent on other commitments.

However, if your research question is not developed by the time you are temporarily drawn away to other commitments, you will not have the assurance that you have a project that is 'do-able' when you resume your review. This could therefore delay your study. There are two main steps you need to take when choosing your research question, which are outlined and explored below.

Step 1: Identify a research topic

The first step in writing your literature review is to decide on a topic that you would like to investigate. If you are undertaking your literature review as a dissertation as part of a professional qualification, you need to ensure that the topic is relevant to the programme for which you are studying. Most professional courses state clearly that the dissertation topic should reflect the general learning outcomes of the programme, so it is important to develop your area of interest so that it reflects the programme on which you are studying. For example, an adult nursing student might be interested to explore the physiological processes involved in heart disease. As this topic has a strong physiological slant, the student would be advised to adapt this to reflect an adult nursing theme. An adaptation could be to explore the role of the nurse in delivering health promotion strategies that would protect against the development of heart disease. This topic has clear relevance to adult nursing, whereas the original topic has a more physiological foundation. In almost every case it will be possible to find an aspect of the chosen topic that reflects the aim of the professional course for which the dissertation is to be submitted, especially when considering the broad knowledge base upon which professional courses are based.

It is critical that the research topic you select is a topic in which you have a genuine interest. Ideally, this will arise from an issue you have become concerned with in your area of professional practice, although this does not have to be the case. An event that occurred in practice, for example, might trigger your interest in exploring a topic. Let's imagine that, as a social work student, you have noticed that clients who use illicit drugs report to you that they get a frosty welcome when they present to the accident and emergency department. You are concerned about whether they are getting as equal access to treatment as other patients and decide to explore this in a literature review. You do need to be aware, however, that if you select a topic about which you are very passionate for whatever reason, you need to remain objective about your literature review from beginning to end. You must resist the temptation to pre-empt the study by having pre-drawn conclusions as to what you will find. You must engage in the literature review using a systematic approach and you may be surprised by the outcomes.

If you are undertaking your literature review as part of a degree, in principle you can build on a topic that has been explored in another area of your course but do check with the university in the first instance, in case you will be penalised for repetition. It is probably reasonable to recommend that no more than 10 per cent of another module/course of study should be repeated in your literature review.

How do I begin to select a good topic?

There are three strategies you can use to develop your interest in a topic for your literature review. First of all, you are advised to read widely around the topics that interest you, in order to develop your thoughts and ideas as to which topic you would like to investigate. It is suggested that you undertake some initial literature searches in order to commence this process. Further discussion of how to search the literature is provided in Chapter 4. You will often get ideas from reading research and other papers that have already been published in the area in which you are interested. You may come across two or more studies on your topic where the results seem very different and this may prompt you to choose to review *all* the literature in this area to find out how these results fit into the literature as a whole. It is wise to ensure that the literature surrounding any potential topic is easily available. If initial searches identify literature that is located in journals that are not stocked by any library that you have access to, then your literature review will be more difficult, as you will be reliant on inter-library loans to access information. Alternatively, the literature surrounding your topic might be easily accessible but might be in journals that you do not normally access. This is not necessarily a disadvantage, however: if you select a topic that has, for example, a medical/pharmaceutical dimension, you may find that you have to negotiate and critique research methods that are unfamiliar to you.

Secondly, discuss your ideas with anyone who will listen to you! For example: peers, friends, health and social care professionals, university tutors. This will help you to clarify and focus your ideas. If you have the opportunity to go to a conference or study day on an area that is closely related to your potential topic area, use this as an opportunity to discuss your ideas with others attending. If you come across research papers in your initial search for literature, email the authors and ask their advice as to which aspect of the topic they feel could be further explored through a literature review. If the topic that interests you derives from your professional practice, discuss this with those who work with you in order to get different perspectives on the topic. Discuss your area of interest with specialist health and social care practitioners working in related fields. Make contact with key people who are working in your area of interest. Explain that you are considering undertaking a project in a particular area and would like to discuss this. In most cases they will be more than happy to discuss their work with you. Even at this stage of the project, keep a diary of everything that you do: the databases you access, the libraries and key words you use and any problems you encounter. You will need this when you come to write up the methods section of your work. You will also find the diary useful if you have to examine your own strengths and limitations and the overall limitations of the approach that you have taken.

Example of a diary: 'I went to see the probation officer about support for young people when they are released from a young offenders' institutions. I discussed my research ideas with him and we discussed the different agencies who are involved and what this impact may be. This has helped me to focus my question towards the role of buddies.'

Thirdly, consider using a mind map. Mind mapping is a process whereby you make notes about your ideas for a literature review question and use these ideas to generate further ideas. In principle, mind mapping is an organised approach to generating ideas from initial ideas that you have. There are many websites available that discuss the concept of mind mapping in great detail which might be useful to access. The general principles are as follows: the main topic is written in the centre of a sheet of paper. You then identify topics that relate directly to the main topic and link these to the main topic. If there are other topics that link in but are less associated with the main topic you can add another layer in your map as in Figure 3.1:

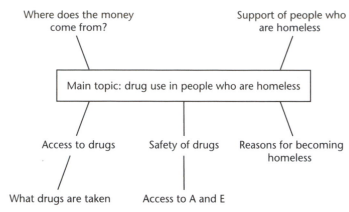

Figure 3.1 Example of a mind map

If you develop a mind map for the topic in which you are interested, you will be able to see how various aspects of the topics relate to each other and how the area you are interested in relates to the topic area as a whole. This will assist you in developing the context for your review.

From these three strategies, you should be able to identify a potential research topic. The next stage is to refine this down into a manageable and workable research question on which your literature review will be based.

Step 2: Identify a research question

Once you have selected your topic of interest, continue reading around this topic to develop your thoughts about possible research questions. The aim of this is to search for unaddressed questions, identify unexplored areas, identify apparent contradictions, find perspectives that have not been considered before or an area in which you have some new ideas.

Questions to be addressed by research can be presented as interrogative or declarative. An interrogative question is stated as a question – for example, 'What factors affect the attrition rate of students from a university course?', whereas a declarative question is written as a statement – for example, 'An investigation of the reasons behind attrition rates from a university course'. It is recommended that you use the interrogative form when framing your research question. That is to ensure that you state a clearly defined research *question* rather than a statement. This will help to ensure that you keep your literature review focussed at all times. It has already been mentioned that the research question provides the context for your entire literature review. It is therefore critical that you follow your chosen question in detail every step of the way. If your research question is phrased as a question, this will enable you to do that. It will be useful to discuss this process in depth with your supervisor.

Rules for writing a good research question

You must be interested and motivated in the topic

Your literature review dissertation usually forms the most substantial component of your degree. It is a long process and will take you many months to complete. It is essential that you pick a topic in which you can maintain your level of interest. You will find that you become an expert on the topic in which your literature review is based. If you are undertaking your literature review as part of a degree, you are likely to find that you will be asked about your review when you attend for job interviews. If you have selected a topic about which you are genuinely interested, you will find it easier to discuss it and might find that what becomes your extensive knowledge of this topic is helpful to you in your future career.

The question should be focussed but not too narrow

A good research question is clear and specific. The remit of the research question should be small – but not too small. If the remit of the research question is too big, you will be inundated with information and you will not be able to review all the information and therefore answer the question. Let's give two examples:

Example 1: *What causes cancer?*

Why is this topic too broad?

The topic is clearly so big that it cannot be tackled by a novice researcher. Indeed, the above question is so vast that a team of researchers could explore this for a lifetime and still leave the question not fully answered! This means that it is unmanageable for a new researcher.

However, the remit of the review should not be so small that there is no identifiable literature to review! Consider the language you use to define the question. Questions beginning with 'how' and 'why' tend to lead to bigger research questions; however, if the topic area is limited then this need not make the question too broad. In general, students have a tendency to have too wide a remit rather than too small, so be prepared to refine the focus of your research question. A more focussed but still too broad a question could be:

> *Are patients aware of the importance of a healthy diet in the prevention of cancer?*

This question is more focussed and could be manageable. In addressing this question, you would have to identify literature that explores patients' perception of healthy lifestyle choices.

Example 2: *What do patients think about their health service?*

Why is this question too broad?

There are many aspects of the health services in any country about which there might be research and other information and the researcher is likely to be deluged with too much information which cannot be processed easily and systematically. Without a large research team and budget, the reviewer would be unlikely to be able to answer this question. The following question is more manageable:

> *What do patients think about restricted visiting times in hospital?*

The focus of this question is patients' thoughts about visiting times and to address this, the reviewer would need to search for research exploring patients' thoughts. This literature is not likely to be extensive and should yield a manageable amount of data to appraise and critique. Any literature regarding the views of relatives and/or staff can be discounted for this review as the remit is fixed. The only area of interest is patients' views.

The question should be clear and unambiguous

The terms referred to in the research question should be clear and unambiguous. You will need to define the terms that you use so that the reader is aware of the specific remit of your work. If, for example, you are looking at a topic about the care of the older person, you need to define how you are using the term 'older person'. You need to define the terms you use – this is sometimes referred to as 'operational definitions'. You then need to make sure that you keep to this remit. It can be tempting to use interesting related literature, which is outside this remit. If this happens, you can use the literature but make sure that you change the definition of the remit of your study at the outset. For example, if you are looking at the role of male health and social care practitioners and you come across interesting ideas that relate to female practitioners, do not be tempted to include this, except in the discussion section, unless you alter the overall remit of your study. This will be discussed in greater detail in Chapter 4.

The question should be answerable and realistic within your time frame

You may have a research question that you are burning to address but if it is too large, or requires resources that are unavailable to you for the timescale you have available, then you will need to scale it down. Remember that your main aim is to pass your dissertation and to demonstrate that you have an understanding of the literature review process. Despite this, many literature reviews undertaken by undergraduate students *do* achieve useful insights into the research question and can lead to publication and enhance your career prospects.

The question should address one (or a maximum of two) key questions only

It is probably realistic at undergraduate level, and even at postgraduate level, to have a question that is short and addresses just one question, or two at most. If you are any more ambitious than this, you are likely not to be able to answer any of the questions satisfactorily. Law (2004) has written a useful and detailed account of developing her research question, describing all the factors that contributed to the final question development. She discusses how her research question for her doctoral study was developed out of her postgraduate-level research and through discussion with those working in the area and extended reading. Clearly for those undertaking smaller scale projects, the question development will be a less protracted process; however, the point to be made is that the development of a question to be addressed by a literature review can be a lengthy process!

The research question should be answerable using the literature

The above criteria relate to the development of all research questions using all methodologies undertaken by novice researchers. However, those undertaking a literature review as their research method of choice need to consider whether the research question is (easily) answerable from the literature. That is, the literature must contain the information that you require to answer the question.

Take, for example, a question which could be given to students taking an advanced-level history exam: 'What were the causes of World War One?' The typical student will diligently access the views and arguments of leading historians and present their analysis of the causes of the war but unless they can access the primary documents on which the debate rests, they will not be able to move the discussion forwards and will be reliant on secondary sources to address their question. In other words, they are not able to address their actual research question. The student is likely to write an extended essay rather than a dissertation. However, if the question was presented as 'What are the differing views of two leading historians as to the causes of the First World War?', then the challenge becomes more realistic – this amended question can be answered using available and accessible literature, as the researcher has only to review the arguments presented by two leading historians. These arguments will be readily available. In principle, those undertaking a literature review should beware of literature review questions that refer to areas of literature which are inaccessible (for example, original documents that are not in the public domain), or so vast that a literature review is not manageable.

Consider the following questions:

Question 1: *What factors contribute to the use of evidence-based practice (EBP) by practitioners in social work?*
Question 2: *What causes patients to self-harm?*

Each of these questions might be addressed by a researcher undertaking primary data collection. Each question could be explored using an exploratory methodology using interviews and/or focus groups to explore these issues with the identified relevant practitioners or patients. However, it would be very different for the researcher who wanted to attempt to address these questions using literature review methodology.

This is because of the availability and accessibility of the relevant material. The use of evidence-based practice is a broad topic and the researcher would have to access a very wide range of literature to identify relevant factors. Furthermore, because of the range of literature, it would be difficult to determine whether the literature had been searched comprehensively. Similarly, the causes of self-harm are complex and this literature would also be difficult to access. These questions could be redefined so that they become manageable to the literature reviewer:

Question 3: *How do social workers refer to and implement evidence-based practice in their day-to-day activity?*

For this revised question, the search for relevant literature is more focussed. The reviewer should search for evidence of the implementation of evidence-based practice rather than any/all 'factors' which might contribute to the use of EBP.

Question 4: *How do practitioners manage patients who self-harm when they present to the accident and emergency department?*

For this revised question, again the search for relevant literature is more focussed. The reviewer should search for literature concerning the management of self-harming patients NA when they are admitted to the accident and emergency department.

Refining the research question

It is very important that, as a new literature reviewer, you can determine whether there is a discrete body of literature which is available to access in order to address the literature review question. While it is theoretically possible to undertake a systematic search of the literature, find that there is very little on your topic and write this up successfully, this is likely to be a frustrating process. Equally, it is theoretically possible to undertake a superficial overview of a vast amount of literature, in which case your critical analysis would be minimal. However, neither of these options is ideal, especially at undergraduate level, where you are likely to be assessed on the *process* you undertook. It is important to demonstrate that you carried out a systematic and comprehensive process in your review. If you have an unmanageable amount of literature, it is unlikely that you will be able to demonstrate a thorough critical appraisal or synthesis of your literature.

For these reasons, it is better to do an initial literature search to assess the scope and variety of literature that has been written on your topic, with special regard to the amount of primary empirical data there is. This will ensure that you are likely to have enough literature to answer your question and will avoid the review becoming an extended essay. If, after carrying out an initial search, there appears to be very little literature on your topic, or if there is extensive literature, you are advised to refine your research question. As a general rule, for a small-scale project at undergraduate level, an ideal range of literature would be no less than six and no more than 15 *research* articles that focus on your topic. Those studying at postgraduate level will be able to utilise more literature. At this initial stage of the project it can be difficult to assess the amount of literature as you will not have undertaken comprehensive searches, but it is important to bear in mind that you do not want to be over-whelmed with literature.

Remind yourself (often) of your question

Once you have identified your research question, you might find it useful to write it down and stick it to your computer screen, fridge, or any surface where you will regularly see it. This will ensure that you do not forget your question and that you are constantly reminded of the focus of the research question. The process of developing a research question can be a lengthy one and will be shaped by what you read and your discussions with others.

Use of a theoretical framework

You may consider, or be asked to consider, using a theoretical framework in order to provide a structure for your literature review. The use of a theoretical framework refers to the application of a particular theory that is relevant to the research question and to which the eventual literature review is referred. Paterson *et al.* (2001) describe the use of a theoretical framework to guide the development of the research question. They argue that it assists the reviewer to define relevant concepts in the litera-ture review research question and to identify the scope of the review. Sometimes a theoretical framework will arise naturally in relation to the research question or even be implicit within the research question. For example, if you were exploring the way in which informed consent is managed in patients undergoing minor surgery, the theory of informed consent would be central to your study and would form a framework around which your study could be based. The results of your literature review would be reviewed in the context of informed consent theory at the end of the study. Alternately, if you were exploring motivation for smoking cessation, you might refer to the stages of change theory (Prochaska *et al.* 1994) and apply the results of your literature to this theory in the discussion.

The incorporation of a theoretical framework into a literature review can be complex. There might not be an apparent theory upon which to frame the study and in this case it is entirely reasonable to proceed with-out a framework. Alternatively, you might actively choose not to restrict the study to a particular framework, but rather to adopt an inductive approach without a pre-existing structure. Thorne (2001) argues that the application of a theoretical framework is not essential to any research study and might have the effect of introducing bias into the study. She argues that researchers might be led in a particular direction because of the framework that is imposed and fail to be responsive to the data that are collected.

For the purpose of a literature review at undergraduate level, students are advised that reference to a theoretical framework is not required unless it is specifically requested by the academic institution in which you are studying. If a theoretical framework is obviously apparent to you as the researcher, as described above, then the underlying theory should be discussed in relation to the research question and then referred to again when the results of the literature review are discussed. If there is no obvious theoretical framework, you should use the research question to frame your literature review. A clearly defined, unambiguous research question will act as a guide to the review. Those undertaking a literature review are advised to define clearly the terms they are using in their review and to articulate clear inclusion and exclusion criteria for litera-ture to be incorporated in the review. This is discussed in Chapter 4.

Reconsideration of your research question

It is important to emphasise that many people refine their question as they go through the process of investigation. This can occur for many reasons. You may encounter an aspect relating to your research topic that interests you more than the aspect to which your original research question relates. You might then change your question to reflect this. You might have difficulties in finding sufficient information that addresses your research question and find more literature relating to a different aspect of your topic area. You might then change your research question so that this literature can be incorporated. This might happen when you are quite a way into your review as it is not always possible to determine how much information is relevant to your review until you have actually read it. This is discussed in Chapter 4. For example, let's say a physiotherapist is interested in evaluating the impact of journal clubs in developing increased research awareness among practitioners. At face value there seems to be no shortage of literature that addresses this topic. However, when this literature is more closely scrutinised, it becomes apparent that there is very little that actually evaluates the impact of the journal clubs. The physiotherapist then broadened the research question to explore whether there is evidence for promoting the concept of a journal club rather than exploring their impact. Reconsidering the scope and title of your research question might not be as disruptive a task as you might think – you are likely to have read widely around the area and will find that the reading you have done can be applied in a different way. If you do change the scope or focus of your research question, you need to make sure that you change the title and that the entire approach to the work reflects the re-worked question.

Writing up the development of your research question

When you come to write up your literature review, you will need to chart the development of your research question, beginning with how you arrived at a topic and how you refined this into a specific question. Be specific about the progress you made and what factors influenced you in this process. For example, if a conversation with a particular person proved to be vital in developing your thoughts, you should document this and the reasons why it was influential. This section is usually included in the methods section of your literature review (for further discussion, please see Chapter 8) and is normally separate from your overall introduction in which you outline the topic area in which you are interested.

Tips for writing up the development of your research question

1 You need to provide a good introduction to your research question, and explain why it is important to you.
2 You need to provide context for your research question. Be prepared to discuss background information that sets your question in its practical, political or theoretical context. Refer to recent relevant government or policy publications.
3 It can be useful to introduce your research question with a description of a critical incident from your practice area which illustrates why the question is important.
4 Remember to document how your research question developed through discussion with experts, email contacts and initial literature searching.
5 Remember to justify why it is appropriate to address your research question through a review of the literature rather than another research method.
6 Once you have developed your question, pin it to the fridge or anywhere you will see it regularly to ensure you address this question.
7 Add your research question to a header or footer to your developing electronic document to help stay focussed.

In summary

Developing a research question can be a difficult and lengthy process but it is important as it provides the structure for the *entire* literature review. A good research question will be focussed and unambiguous, stimulating to the researcher, relevant to their area of clinical practice and achievable within the time frame. It should also be answerable from the literature. It is always good advice to write out the research question and place it in a location where you will read it often. Put your research question as a header on your documents on your computer so that you refer to it constantly. This will help you make sure that you are still answering your question and that your question does not need to be redefined. There are three main processes in the research methodology for a literature review that need to be adhered to when developing a systematic approach to addressing the research question. These three processes are addressed in the next three chapters: searching for literature (collecting data), critiquing the literature (Chapter 5) and synthesising the literature (Chapter 6).

Key points

- Identifying a research question is a key process in the literature review methodology.
- The idea behind the question will ideally originate from your practice area and should interest you.
- Research questions should be focussed, manageable and answerable from the available literature.

4

How do I search for literature?

Developing a systematic approach to searching for literature • What exactly are you trying to find out in your literature review? • Inclusion and exclusion criteria • Using the right evidence to answer your question • Methods of searching the literature • Electronic searching • Searching electronic databases • Recording your searching strategy • Additional methods of identifying relevant articles • Use of abstracts to confirm the relevance of the paper • Getting hold of your references • Strengths and limitations of your searching strategy • Tips for writing up your search strategy • In summary • Key points

Once you have established the research question that can be answered from the available literature, you need to develop a search strategy that will enable you to identify and locate the widest range of published material that is relevant to your research topic and that will enable you to address the research question. This is essential to ensure that you identify as much of the literature that is relevant to your review as possible, within the time and financial restrictions of your review.

Developing a systematic approach to searching for literature

This is a key area – a literature review that is approached systematically is very different from one that is approached in a haphazard manner. A thorough and comprehensive search strategy will help to ensure that you identify key literature/texts on your topic and that you will find the relevant research that has been undertaken in your area. Without a thorough search strategy, your searching will be random and disorganised and the reader of the review will not be confident that you have identified all the relevant research papers relating to your topic.

What *exactly* are you trying to find out in your literature review?

The first step is to articulate clearly the focus of literature that you will seek in order to answer your question. This is important in order to ensure that you follow your research question closely throughout the review and obtain only that information which is relevant to the research question in your search for literature. Remember that it is very easy to get sidetracked when you are searching for literature. For example, if you are interested in exploring students' experience of illicit drug use at university, you need to have a strategy for identifying this specific literature rather than related but more general literature which does not address your research question, for example literature exploring the effect of a conviction for illicit drug use on future career prospects.

You need to be able to develop a strategy for managing the literature so that you can identify quickly which literature is directly related to your research question, and which is not. Literature that is not relevant to you must be discarded in the first instance. You might return to this literature at a later stage but it should not be incorporated in the review if it does not directly address the research question. In order to identify the types of literature you need to answer your question, it is important to develop inclusion and exclusion criteria for your literature review.

Inclusion and exclusion criteria

Inclusion and exclusion criteria enable the literature reviewer to identify the literature that addresses the research question and that which does not. The criteria you develop will be guided by the wording of your research question and will enable you to articulate the focus of your research. Unless your question clearly indicates otherwise, you will normally be looking for primary research on your topic in the first instance. This is because primary research provides the research findings from a study and is reported first-hand. You might find that primary research is reported in other articles but you will not get the full account of the research unless you go straight to the primary source. Primary research is most often published in journals and you will tend to find the most up-to-date resources on your topic in journal articles rather than in textbooks. This is because the subject matter of most textbooks tends to be quite broad and is quickly out of date. This is discussed in more detail in Chapter 5. The inclusion and exclusion criteria will be specific to your individual literature review but examples of appropriate inclusion and exclusion criteria might be as follows:

- Example of inclusion criteria:
  - Primary research directly related to the topic
  - English language only
  - Published literature only
  - 1985 onwards
- Example of exclusion criteria:
  - Primary research not directly related to the topic area
  - Not English language
  - Unpublished research
  - Pre-1985

The main rationale for setting your inclusion and exclusion criteria is to focus your literature searching and to ensure that you do not get sidetracked with data that are not strictly relevant to your review. Thus setting appropriate criteria assists you in keeping your study focussed. If you have pre-determined what information you need you will be able to identify what is relevant to you more easily than if you have not thought this through. However, you will find that some of your criteria are set for practical reasons, given that you will have a limited time frame within which to search and undertake your review. For example, you are likely to limit your search to more recent literature and to omit unpublished literature from your review. Neither of these restrictions is ideal and, under optimum conditions, you would obtain all available literature that is related to your topic. For example, there might be a seminal piece of work which is highly relevant to your review but which was published before the date limitations you set. If you set time restrictions to your search for literature you would miss this seminal document, although of course it might be referred to in other papers that you encounter. There is also concern about reviewing only literature that has been published. This is because of the risk of publication bias – that is journals tend to publish research that shows the positive effect of an intervention rather than a negative effect or no effect (Easterbrook *et al.* 1991). Hence only including published literature could bias your review. There might be a lot of 'hidden' evidence about your topic that remains unpublished because the results showed no effect. This literature is often referred to as 'grey' literature and refers to literature that is not published or generally in the public domain, for example an unpublished study or dissertation. Non-academic journals might also be referred to as grey literature and other information such as hospital policies also fall into this category. As a novice researcher you would not be expected to access 'grey' literature which is difficult to find. Unpublished literature can be hard to identify or get hold of. Searching for unpublished, or grey, literature will usually be beyond the scope of the literature reviewer at undergraduate level as the researcher is unlikely to have the time and resources to search for unpublished research. If this is the case then it needs to be mentioned when you discuss the limitations of your review methodology.

In reality your inclusion and exclusion criteria will be a combination of limits that are necessary to focus your search and pragmatic limitations which are required due to the resources available to you. The important point is that you are able to justify why you have set the inclusion and exclusion criteria, which should be determined by the needs of your review rather than your own convenience. For example, it would not be appropriate to include only those studies which you can access electronically if a hard-bound copy of an article you require is available in the local library.

It is important to refer frequently to these inclusion and exclusion criteria throughout your searching. It is also important to keep checking that these criteria remain relevant to your research question – you may need to amend either or both of these as your literature review progresses. You need to make sure that you do not get sidetracked by interesting but peripheral issues if these are not directly related to your research question. However, if you encounter an interesting angle to the literature you are searching and decide to change your research question so that this can be incorporated, then this can be appropriate.

Using the right evidence to answer your question

While refining your searching strategy, you may be able to identify the types of literature and research that will be most useful to you in answering your question. This will depend on your research question. A few examples are given below to illustrate this:

Example A

You are doing a literature review exploring the effectiveness of a particular treatment or intervention, and as a result, the literature that is generally considered to be most useful to you in answering this question will be randomised controlled trials (RCTs). This is because this research design is recognised as the 'gold standard' approach to determining the effectiveness of a particular treatment because of the comparison that is possible between the intervention and control group, as discussed in Chapter 2. You should therefore search for RCTs in the first instance. These are likely to provide the best and most reliable evidence with which you can address your question. However, that is not to say that RCTs are the only type of literature you should seek to identify. It might be that RCTs were not an appropriate method for exploring the topic area you have identified. There might be cohort studies or case control studies that provide the most appropriate evidence. You would need to explore which type of studies are most suitable for addressing your research question. Evans (2003) identifies that RCTs provide strong internal validity for a study – that is, the difference in outcomes between the two groups is highly likely to be attributable to the intervention due to the controlled nature of the study. However, because of the strict protocols for inclusion in the study, RCTs are usually carried out on select groups of patients who qualify for inclusion. Observational studies such as cohort studies and case control studies are less well controlled and are therefore likely to provide greater external validity – that is, the results have greater generalisability because the studies observe what is happening in practice. However, because the groups are not randomly allocated, it is not possible to determine whether differences in outcome between groups are due to the intervention.

Example B

You are doing a literature review to explore students' perceptions of their time at university, which means you are likely to be looking for cross-sectional studies (surveys and questionnaires) and qualitative approaches. You would need to be aware that questionnaires will obtain a different type of data to that obtained by in-depth qualitative interviews.

Example C

You are doing a literature review to explore whether students comply with handwashing procedures in clinical practice, and so you are likely to be searching for research in which direct observation has been employed as the main method in the first instance. This is because indirect reports of handwashing practices, for example question-naire/surveys, report what practitioners say they do rather than what they actually do. You would search for indirect reports of handwashing practice as a second line of evidence.

You will note from examples A, B and C cited above, that the literature that is most useful in answering the research question in each case has been empirical research evidence. Therefore, you should give most weight to the relevant empirical research that addresses the research question in your review. However, this will not always be the case. Consider the following example:

Example D

You are doing a literature review to explore how the media reports health and social care issues – for example, the MMR scare. To answer this question, the literature that will be most useful to you will be the media reports themselves. You are likely to write an introductory chapter on the importance of MMR, but your research question can only be answered by searching for and analysing media reports. In this case, you would not search for research in the first instance as this would not help you to address the research question directly.

While understanding which research approaches are most likely to be relevant to answering your research question, you are advised to remain open minded at this stage about the inclusion of all types of information if they are relevant to your research question, otherwise you risk losing important data (Lloyd-Jones 2004).

In Chapter 2, the concept of a hierarchy of evidence was introduced, in which the evidence that is most useful in determining the effectiveness of treatments or interventions is ranked. It was emphasised that this particular hierarchy only ranks evidence about the effectiveness of treatments or interventions as in Example A. As the examples above illustrate, different types of evidence are important for different types of questions in a literature review. You might find it useful to develop your own 'hierarchy of evidence' for ranking the types of evidence that you need to address the research question for your literature review, as illustrated in the examples above. Think carefully about the type of evidence you need to address your research question and run your ideas by your peers and of course your research supervisor. You are then advised to concentrate your initial searches for this type of evidence in the first instance. You should write up your rationale for doing this in your methods section of your literature review.

Methods of searching the literature

Once you have established your search strategy you are ready to start searching. Before you begin, however, consider how you are going to manage the references you identify. It is vitally important to back up all your records and keep them in a safe place from the moment that you begin the searching process. If you are keeping records on a computer remember to have a back-up copy at all times. Keep all of them up-to-date. Keep track of your references, write them down in full every time you read something useful. It is very frustrating to have to track down page numbers or editions at the last minute just because you used something in the write-up that you hadn't anticipated including. Think about keeping a card file with all your references, set out according to the reference style set by your university or college of higher education. You could add a sentence that will remind you of the content of the paper and file them according to chapter headings. As you use them in the write-up you could then file them in alphabetical order ready for your reference section at the end, or you could file them under the chapter headings in which you anticipate using them.

There are four main ways of searching for literature. These are electronic searching using computer-held databases, searching reference lists, hand searching relevant journals specific to the research topic and contacting authors directly. These four approaches will be considered in turn.

Electronic searching

Searching for literature when undertaking a literature review has been revolutionised in recent years by the advances in **electronic databases**. In years gone by, those reviewing the literature would have to search through hard-bound volumes of subject-indexed references in which previously published literature was categorised. Clearly these volumes could not be immediately updated as to do so required a reprint of the entire publication, which took place often on a yearly basis. Searching for literature has become a far easier and efficient process with the advent of electronic databases for literature searching.

Computerised databases are huge subject indexes of journal articles and other literature related to the topic for which you are searching. Various databases will be available through the university or hospital library to which you belong. The first step is to identify databases to which you have access and to establish the relevance of these for the searching strategy. Commonly held databases include:

- Allied and Alternative Medicine (AMED)
- Applied Social Sciences Index and Abstracts (ASSIA)
- British Nursing Index (BNI)
- CANCER-CD
- Caredata
- Cochrane Library
- Cumulative Index to Nursing and Allied Health Literature (CINAHL)
- DHSS-DATA
- Dissertation Abstracts
- Index to Theses
- Medline
- PsycLit
- PsycINFO
- Social Care Online
- Social Services Abstracts
- Sociofile
- System for Information on Grey Literature in Europe

For those undertaking a nursing-based literature review, CINAHL would be an appropriate start. CINAHL covers a wide range of international nursing literature, commencing in 1982. There are various different searching strategies which include, for example, the possibility to search for research articles only. For those undertaking social work-based studies, Social Care Online is a good place to start. MEDLINE is a more generic database, offering reference to medical, nursing and social care literature. It is important to note that while MEDLINE is a huge database, it contains reference to journal articles only, whereas other databases such as CINAHL reference a wider range of book and non-research information, in addition to journal articles. In principle, all those undertaking a review of the literature are strongly recommended to consult with the academic subject librarian at their university for further advice concerning the appropriate use of databases for a particular study.

Searching electronic databases

The process of searching each of these databases will vary from one to another and you are advised to seek appropriate assistance from your academic subject librarian to do so. The general principles are as follows. In the first instance you should identify the keywords that capture the essence of the research topic or research question for the review. You should be as creative as possible at this stage as the topic or question might be categorised in different ways by different researchers. You also need to consider whether there are different meanings to the keywords that you identify in different countries, especially given that databases have different biases. For example, CINAHL has a strong North American bias, the BNI has a British focus. It is also wise to remember that you may identify new keywords as you progress with your searching and encounter alternative ways in which your research topic is represented in the literature. You will find that you identify new possible search terms as your searching progresses.

When you have made a list of a few possible keywords for each aspect of your topic, you are ready to start searching. Make sure you make use of the AND/OR commands in the searching strategy as appropriate. AND ensures that both terms you have entered are searched for, whereas OR ensures that either one term or another is selected. These commands use the principles of Boolean logic. In addition, there is also the * facility which enables you to identify all possible endings of the key term you write. For example nurs* will identify articles containing nurse, nursing, nurses and so on. You can also specify whether you would like to search throughout the whole article for the term, or whether you are going to limit your search to the **abstract** or title. Clearly if you limit your search to the identification of the term in just the title, you will exclude a lot of references which might be relevant to you, even though the title does not use the key terms you have identified. Conversely, if you search through the whole articles for your keyword, you are likely to be over-whelmed with literature. Limiting your search to the abstract is likely to be a suitable compromise. Littleton *et al.* (2004) provide a detailed guide to literature searching in their publication, *Searching the literature by design*, which is a useful reference.

You are advised to continue searching the databases, refining your searching strategy as you progress. You are likely to find that you develop new ideas for the search terms you use as you start the searching process. You might find, for example, a key theme is called by a different name or phrase that you had not previously thought of. Be aware of this and be prepared to search using new and different terms. Remember as well to keep a record of the search terms you have used and the results of these searches. If you do not have any 'hits' from your search, then you need to keep searching with different keywords until you identify litera-ture which is linked to your topic area. If you have too many hits, you will need to refocus your search.

Once you have identified the key literature on your topic using one database, you should repeat the search using another database. If you find that the same references are thrown up, then you can be confident that your strategy is well focussed and that you are accessing the rele-vant literature on your topic. You might feel it is appropriate to scale down your search. Discuss this with your supervisor. If new references are constantly being thrown up, you will need to continue searching until later searches reveal little or no new information. This is where the importance of having a research question that is neither too big nor too small is evident. Ideally you will retrieve 10–20 references that are well focussed on your topic. As mentioned previously, it would be difficult to address your research question with fewer references but you would be inundated with literature if many more references were identified.

Recording your searching strategy

Once you have undertaken a systematic electronic literature search and have accessed these references, you should have a reasonable selection of articles which are relevant to your research question. You should also keep a record of your searching strategy and the keywords that you used, so that you can demonstrate a systematic approach that is the most likely to yield relevant literature for your topic. For example, if you are searching for primary research articles concerned with sexual health and nursing care in hospital, you might initially undertake two basic searches and then combine these searches:

Databases: CINAHL 1994– Search term: sexual*:
Total number of hits: 30,000

Databases: CINAHL 1994– Search term: sexual* AND nurs*
Total number of hits: 15,000

You can then demonstrate how you combined this search with another search in order to obtain a more manageable number of hits.

It is important that you demonstrate the success of your searching strategy and which searches yielded the best results. It is also useful to state what type of literature your hits included, if you can determine this from the abstract available. If you are searching for articles of primary research but are failing to identify these, you need to document this. This enables the reader to develop a sense of the ease with which you were able to identify literature and the outcome of your searches. For example, if you were to state that you identified 2000 articles that were relevant to your topic area and met your inclusion criteria, but then continued to review just 20 of these, the reader would be left unaware as to how you refined your search from such a large number of hits down to 20 and whether you had omitted relevant articles in the process. You need to document the process of refining down your search so that the reader is satisfied that relevant papers have not been omitted on the way.

Additional methods of identifying relevant articles

It should be emphasised that, despite the advances in electronic searching, computerised searching tools are not 100 per cent comprehensive and will fail to identify relevant literature on your topic. This is because some relevant literature might have been categorised using different keywords and therefore would not be identified by one particular searching strategy. Evans (2002) noted how the relevance and focus of many studies was not identifiable through the title alone, indicating that it is easily possible to miss studies that are critical to your research question because the focus of the study is not immediately apparent. Hawker *et al.* (2002) identify how authors who use humorous titles for their work run the risk that their work will not be identified by those who search on the topic. Although using various keywords will help identify literature that is not identified on the first search, it is still possible for literature to remain unidentified even though it is highly relevant to addressing the research question. Montori *et al.* (2004) undertook electronic searching for their literature review and describe how they frequently came across relevant literature by chance that had not been identified through their comprehensive electronic searching strategy. For this reason, electronic searches are likely to be the main component of your search strategy, but not the only component. It is important to remember that there is no single strategy that will ensure that you retrieve all the information you need to address your research question. Further strategies including reference list searching, hand searching through reference lists and author searching, will add to the thoroughness of your searching strategy.

Greenhalgh and Peacock (2005) emphasise the importance of using many approaches to identifying appropriate literature when undertaking a literature search and argue that systematic reviewers cannot rely on computerised databases to yield all the information they need for their study. It may seem haphazard to employ a variety of methods to search for literature, especially if these appear somewhat random, such as scrutinising recent copies of particular journals. However, given the limitations of using electronic searching alone, the wider searching strategy, as long as it is organised and its relevance is justified in the remit of the study, can be part of a comprehensive systematic approach. Greenhalgh and Peacock refer to this process as **snowball sampling** – where the sampling strategy develops according to the requirements of the study and is responsive to the literature already obtained. For example, if useful articles are found in a particular journal, then this journal is further scrutinised for other relevant material. This strategy cannot be pre-specified and is dependent on the results of early literature searching. Greenhalgh and Peacock (2005) reported 'snowball sampling' to be the most effective approach to literature searching in their systematic review.

Searching the reference lists

Once you have identified the key articles that relate to your research question, it is useful to scrutinise the reference lists of those key articles for further references that may be useful to you.

Hand searching relevant journals

If you have been able to identify that many of your key articles which are relevant to your research question are located in one or two journals, it might be useful to you to hand search these journals to see whether you can identify other relevant articles that have not been identified through other searching strategies. Searching through the contents pages of these journals may identify other relevant material.

Author searching

The same principle applies to author searching. If you find that many of your key articles are by the same author(s) then it may be useful to carry out an author search in order to identify whether the author(s) have published other work which has not been identified in the electronic search. This might also lead you towards work in progress.

A combination of these strategies will ensure that you have the most comprehensive search strategy and therefore the most chance of retrieving the information that is relevant to your research question. However, you can never be certain that you have obtained all the literature on a particular topic. For this reason, it is recommended that you avoid statements that declare that there is no literature on a particular topic and state instead that no literature *was identified* on the topic in question.

Use of abstracts to confirm the relevance of the paper

The next step is to sort through the reference list you now have and identify which references are most relevant to your research question. To do this, you cannot rely on the title alone. This is because the focus of the article – and even whether or not it is a primary research study – is often unclear from the title alone. Barroso *et al.* (2003) and Evans (2002) found that use of the title alone to determine the relevance of a study to their particular research questions was not efficient. Studies were included which, on retrieval of the article, were found to be irrelevant. Similarly, studies were excluded by title alone when on later retrieval, they were found to be relevant. Rather than rely on the title to determine the relevance of a paper to your literature review question, it is preferable to read the abstract for each reference you have identified. The abstract will give you a summary of the content of the article, in particular whether it is a research article or not. The abstract is often available on electronic databases such as CINAHL or MEDLINE. However, abstracts can themselves be unreliable sources for determining the exact focus of a paper, and you might find that you miss relevant literature if you discard a paper because of the information contained in the abstract. Although given that you are unlikely to be able to access in full each paper you identify from an electronic search, it is likely that you will have to rely on the abstract to determine whether or not you include a paper in your literature review. You can document this when you write up the limitations of the approach you have taken.

Once you have accessed the abstracts for your references, refer back to the inclusion and exclusion criteria you have set for your study and assess each of the abstracts according to the perceived relevance for your study. You can then determine which references meet your criteria and which do not. Retain those which do and discard those which clearly do not. If you cannot tell from the abstract, you will need to access the paper in order to do this. By undertaking this process, you should be able to edit your reference lists to those articles and information which are directly relevant to your research question. You can now use this edited reference list to locate the articles that are relevant to your research question.

Getting hold of your references

The references to which you are directed are likely to be found in journals, books and other publications. Your academic subject librarian will be able to help you locate publications with which you are not familiar. Most university libraries will have many journals accessible electronically and you will find that you can locate and download many articles without leaving your computer. The on-line journals will be available from your library website but will be at different databases from those accessed to identify the literature. You are strongly advised to familiarise yourself with the journals to which you have easy access through your library. If the reference you require is not available electronically, then you will need to access the bound volumes which are available as hard copies in the library. If the references which are vital to your research question are not available electronically or in bound volumes in your local library, then you will either need to arrange to visit another library or arrange an inter-library loan. It is important to remember that obtaining these references can be expensive and time consuming so you will need to make a decision about the effort you are going to go to, to access the references you need. For those references which are of interest to, but not crucial to your research question, and which are not easily available, it is reasonable to explain in your methodology that the retrieval of these articles was not possible due to the time and financial limitations of the study. However, you will be given credit for the effort you make in obtaining key references for your literature review.

Strengths and limitations of your searching strategy

Clearly, those doing a more detailed systematic review would make every effort to retrieve the articles relevant to their study. Overall, you will be given credit for the effort you make in locating all the references that are central to your study; however, you will not be unduly penalised if you cannot get hold of hard-to-reach articles which are not critical in answering your research question. You should, however, write this up in your methodology section as a potential limitation of your study.

Another limitation of undertaking a literature review by one novice researcher is also apparent at this point. If you were undertaking a more detailed systematic review, it would be usual for a team of researchers to review each of the identified references and review its relevance for the literature review (Paterson *et al.* 2001). The novice researcher is disadvantaged because these resources are unlikely to be available to them. This should also be discussed in the method section of the literature review.

It should also be emphasised that you should never be tempted to use sources in your literature review if you have not read the source in its original form. If an interesting reference is referred to in another research paper, but the reference is hard to access, you should never attempt to incorporate this material into your review. It is better to cite the reference and explain that you were unable to obtain it than to pretend that you have. This is because without reading the original document, you are unable to critique the material (as described in the following chapter) and are likely to misrepresent the material. If you use secondary sources, the entire foundation for your literature review is challenged as the importance of undertaking a review is that you pull together the available literature and critique it for relevance to your research question. The use of secondary sources was discussed in Chapter 2 and you are advised to avoid using secondary sources wherever possible.

Tips for writing up your search strategy

1 Remember that the aim of this section is to demonstrate how you undertook a systematic approach to your searching.
2 Discuss the approach you took to develop effective search strategies.
3 Keep a record of all the search terms used so that you can provide evidence of your approach.
4 Keep a record of the other approaches you employed to search for literature.
5 Be able to comment on the effectiveness of the approaches you used. For example, if electronic searching did not yield as many hits as you had hoped, discuss why this might have been.
6 Make every effort to obtain relevant literature.
7 It is more accurate to write 'I did not find any literature on X' rather than state categorically 'There is no literature on X'.

In summary

You should by now be well aware of the importance of a systematic search strategy. This will ensure that you access a comprehensive range of literature that is relevant to your literature review question. The use of inclusion and exclusion criteria is also vital to ensure that the literature identified is relevant to your review question. The need to combine the electronic searching of relevant databases with additional strategies such as hand searching journals and reference lists has been discussed. You need to be aware that electronic searching can never be fully comprehensive and that 'snowball sampling', using many different strategies to identify literature will usually be the most effective way of achieving the most comprehensive literature search. At the end of the searching process, you will achieve a list of references that are relevant to your research question for your literature review, which you will be able to locate in your academic library. You will be given credit for the amount of effort you make in accessing these references.

At this point, you should be confident that you have identified the most relevant literature that will enable you to answer your research question. You should be aware of the strengths and limitations of your search strategy. It is now time to stand back and take a critical look at the literature you have identified. Ideally, you will have identified between 10 and 20 references that are key to your research question. If you have many more than this or far fewer you may consider altering the focus of your review so that the literature you have identified fits your research question rather than vice versa. This is a luxury that you have if you are undertaking your literature review as part of an academic degree which you would not have with more formally commissioned research. The main point to remember is that your literature should address your research question. While theoretically you could write up a study which yielded no results, you will find it easier – and more interesting – to write up a study that did yield you some information. If you do not have sufficient information to address your research question, you are advised to alter your question so that you can address it using the literature that you have identified.

Key points

- You should identify the types of literature that will enable you to answer your research question.
- Inclusion and exclusion criteria should be specific to your literature review.
- The literature search strategy should incorporate a variety of approaches including electronic searching, hand searching and reference list searching.
- The limitations of these approaches should be acknowledged.

5

How do I critically appraise the literature?

Getting to know your literature

Once you have completed a comprehensive search for the published material and obtained the literature that is deemed to be relevant to your chosen research question, the next step is to **read** and **re-read** the material so that you become familiar with everything that you have and you can then begin to determine the strengths, limitations and relevance of the information. At this point, you should be able to discuss with confidence the content of your research papers and other information with your research supervisor.

This is important because, in addition to knowing your papers well, you need to evaluate the contribution that each reference makes to answering your research question. To do this, you need to study carefully the research methods used in each research paper that you have. You then need to make a decision about the importance of the research to your particular research question. For example, at first glance, a research paper might appear to address your research question directly; however, on closer inspection you realise that the scope of the paper is very different from what your initial assessment had led you to believe and in fact has only indirect relevance to your research question. Alternatively, you might find that although the context of the paper is relevant to your research question, the methods used in the paper have been poorly carried out and consequently you are less confident in the results of the study. **Critical appraisal** of each individual research paper is therefore very important and will enable you to make assessments as to the relevance of the paper to your study, in addition to identifying the strengths and limitations – and therefore the impact – that the paper will have on addressing your research question. In short, at this point in your literature review, you need to examine carefully all of the information you have identified for relevance to your research question and quality of information provided.

The importance of critical appraisal

The controversy surrounding the MMR vaccination discussed in Chapter 1 illustrates the importance of undertaking critical appraisal of all research and other information that you encounter. In 1998,

Wakefield and his colleagues published a paper in the leading international academic medical journal *The Lancet*, which caused much concern and controversy. It should be noted that this paper has subsequently been withdrawn by *The Lancet*. In this paper, Wakefield *et al.* described how they investigated a series of 12 children who had been referred to their paediatric gastroenterology unit with a history of normal development followed by loss of acquired skills including language, as well as suffering from diarrhoea and abdominal pains. The parents reported that the onset of symptoms was associated with the administration of the MMR vaccination in 8 of the 12 children and with measles infection in another child. Wakefield and colleagues concluded that the potential link between autism and bowel disease with the MMR vaccination should be investigated.

This paper caused huge concern among the general public and the possibility of a link between the MMR vaccination, autism and bowel disease was speculated upon throughout the media. The importance of critical appraisal of this paper cannot be overemphasised here. If you look back to the hierarchy of evidence discussed in Chapter 2, you would probably rank it as little more than expert opinion or anecdotal evidence given the size of the sample and lack of a comparison group. You would probably therefore conclude that the evidence for a link between the MMR vaccination and autism/bowel disease is weak and you would not consider acting on this weak evidence in your clinical practice. Yet, it is unfortunate that such critical appraisal did not halt the media scare that ensued, which resulted in many parents not presenting their children for vaccination and the vaccination rate dropped dangerously low. As a result of this scare, many further studies were undertaken and no further evidence has been found to substantiate Wakefield's claims. Finally, these studies were incorporated into a systematic review which again found no evidence of a link between MMR vaccination and autism/bowel disease.

The MMR controversy illustrates the importance of critical appraisal of research and other information so that you can identify how strong and relevant the evidence is relating to a particular topic. In this chapter the topic of critical appraisal will be discussed.

What is critical appraisal?

Critical appraisal is the structured process of examining a piece of research in order to determine its strengths and limitations, and therefore the weight it should have in your literature review. In principle, all the published material you use in your literature review should be critiqued for relevance and its strengths and limitations. You should never cite an author without some analysis of the contribution this author makes to your debate, unless you are summarising well known arguments at the beginning of your literature review, or summarising arguments in your discussion.

Those new to academic writing often fall into one of two categories. The first accept any piece of research or other information at face value and so accept what is written without question. They cite a reference without any statement about the quality or authenticity of the report. In writing a literature review, this is not appropriate because it is essential to analyse the quality of the information in order to determine the contribution of the information to the overall argument. Those new to academic discussion may perceive a paper that is published in a reputable journal to be above critique and so do not attempt any structured appraisal of the paper. Yet the MMR paper published in *The Lancet* clearly demonstrates that this is not the case. Even a paper that is published in a reputable journal must be examined for the relevance that it demonstrates to the topic area. The second category interpret the term 'critical appraisal' to mean that they must criticise and find fault with everything that they read. They feel that unless they demonstrably 'tear to pieces' what they find, then they have not done their job. It should be noted that while it is possible to find faults with every piece of research, it needs to be remembered that no research is perfect. If only perfect research was included in a literature review, there would be no reviews at all!

Critical appraisal is one of the most important features of a literature review that distinguishes the review from a more traditional essay. Those undertaking a literature review should resist the temptation merely to make a statement and then to provide a reference that apparently reinforces this statement. If no other information is given about the reference that allegedly makes this assertion, the reader has no evidence that this reference is used appropriately.

To give a *bad* hypothetical example: 'Smith (2006) argues that university students prefer lectures to tutorials'. If this is the only information that is given, the reader is unaware of the context from which the author is writing. It is unclear whether the author is merely citing an opinion or referring to published research or whether the paper is actually the report of empirical findings about students' learning preferences. Further information needs to be given.

To give another hypothetical example: 'In a questionnaire survey of 2000 students in London, Smith (2006) identified that 70 per cent of university students preferred . . .' You would then go on to include the strengths and limitations of this survey. For example, you would need to state that only 20 per cent of students responded and of those who did respond, many of them did not fully complete the questionnaire. You may then conclude that the data suggesting that 70 per cent of students preferred a certain learning style is not very strong evidence. Alternatively, if the article by Smith (2006) is actually an account of the author's own preference at university, you might then articulate this as follows: 'Smith (2006) argues that from his own experience as a student in London, there was strong feeling among his peer group that lectures were preferable to seminars'. You then make it clear that Smith is not referring to a piece of empirical research but to his own experience. Having identified the context of Smith's argument, you then need to explore the relevance of his argument to your own research question and whether the students to whom Smith is referring are similar to those you are interested in.

Do I need to critically appraise *all* the literature I include in my review?

Throughout the process of undertaking your literature review, you are strongly encouraged to critically appraise the information you use so that the reader can identify the context of the information you have included. However, this is generally not required in the introductory section of your literature in which you are rehearsing well established arguments and setting the context for your own review. In this case, you do not need to evaluate all the evidence. You can simply cite an appropriate reference. For example, suppose you are doing a literature review to evaluate the perception of smokers on the health risks associated with smoking. In your introduction, you are likely to discuss what is known about the link between smoking and ill health. As this is background information to your research question, you do not need to evaluate this evidence, but can accept it at face value. You could state, for example, that 'It is well established that smoking causes lung cancer (Doll and Hill 1954)'. This is background information, that is well established in the literature and you are not questioning this. You only need to start your critical appraisal when you begin to examine the literature that relates specifically to addressing your research question. However, you do need to ensure that the reference you cite is appropriate to the point you are making. If you are citing a commonly held fact, try to trace back to the origin of this information and cite an appropriate reference, as illustrated above.

Getting started with critical appraisal

The first step in the critical appraisal process is to identify what is happening in the research papers and other information you have. Start getting to know your literature. At this point it is normal to feel swamped by the amount of literature. It may help you to write down the main findings and arguments presented in each paper.

Separate research papers from discussion/opinion papers

You are advised to collect your references together and identify what is a research paper and what is a discussion paper or other information. Depending on the focus of your research question, research papers will normally provide stronger evidence in addressing your question than other papers that you have, but in any case, you need to be clear what types of literature you have. Research papers normally begin with a specific research question which is addressed using an identified method, following which the results and conclusions are recorded and discussed.

Overall, you will probably have a combination of qualitative and quantitative research, maybe some systematic reviews and other non-research information for incorporation into your literature review. Group your literature together so that you have all the qualitative research papers in one pile, the quantitative papers in another and so on. When you have done this, you will be able to identify the types of literature you have for critical review and you will then be able to select the appropriate method of critical appraisal for the literature that you have. The next step is to get to know your literature. Read each paper several times until you can summarise what is going on in each paper. Ask yourself why the study was undertaken or why the paper was written. Then, if the paper reports a research study, you can ask yourself how the study was conducted and what the main results were. You need to be familiar with all the material that you have before you can move on to more detailed critical appraisal. It is always a good test of how well you know the literature if you can discuss the literature you have found in detail with your research supervisor without reference to the papers themselves or at least with minimal reference!

Once you have become familiar with your literature, the next step is to decide how you will critically appraise the literature that you have.

Critical appraisal tools

In order to facilitate the process of critical appraisal, there are many **critical appraisal tools** available to guide the evaluation of research. You are advised to use a critical appraisal tool to assist you in the critique of your research, as they will guide you through questions you need to ask of each paper you have. These tools are frequently used by those reviewing research and there are many different tools available both on the internet, for example the Critical Appraisal Skills Programme (CASP) at www.phru.nhs.uk/casp/casp.htm, and in research textbooks, for example *Essentials of Nursing Research* by Polit and Beck (2005). Most of the critical appraisal tools that you encounter are designed to appraise empirical research, but there are recognised approaches for evaluating the strengths and limitations of non-research papers. Tools and assessment strategies are also available for assessing the quality of published material that does not fall under the category of empirical research, but these are less well developed. Methods for approaching the critical appraisal of non research papers are discussed at the end of the chapter.

Which appraisal tool should I use?

There are a wide range of appraisal tools available. This raises the issue of which tool to use for a particular paper. One study identified 121 published critical appraisal tools located on the internet and in electronic databases (Katrak *et al*. 2004). Many critical appraisal tools have been developed for the review of specific types of research, and as such are design specific, for example, for the review of randomised controlled trials only. Other critical appraisal tools are generic and suitable for all types of research. At first glance, the reviewer might be tempted to use a critical appraisal tool that is generic to all types of research, especially if the literature searching strategy has identified many different approaches to research. However, the reviewer does need to assess the quality and appropriate application of the critical appraisal tool. For example, Katrak *et al.* (2004) found that although 121 different tools had been identified, the effectiveness of these tools in identifying the strengths and limitations of studies had only been evaluated in a few cases. The consequence of this is that it is difficult for those who use research to be confident that the tools they use are 'fit for purpose'. They concluded that there is no 'gold standard' for the critical appraisal of research papers, but rather a lack of information available on the development and validity of the tools that exist.

Critical appraisal for new researchers

Most researchers recommend the use of a critical appraisal tool in order to develop a consistent approach to the critique of research and other information (Oxman 1994, MacAuley *et al.* 1998). It could be argued that the use of an appropriate appraisal tool to critique the research papers is not essential, especially if you have in-depth knowledge of a particular research approach used in the paper; however, the review process is complex and use of an appraisal tool will assist in the development of a systematic approach to this process and ensure that all papers are reviewed with equal rigour. If you are reviewing the literature for the first time and do not have an in-depth understanding of the research approaches adopted in the studies, the use of a critical appraisal tool is strongly recommended.

Furthermore, novice researchers are advised to use a critical appraisal tool that is specific to the type of research they are reviewing rather than a generic critical appraisal tool. This is because the questions will be closely related to the specific study design in question, providing an appropriate structure for the review.

It is important to note that using a critical appraisal tool will not help you if you do not understand the fundamental principles of the research design of the study you are critiquing. It is therefore important to become familiar with the basic research methods of the research papers you have identified. If you do not understand the research methods used by the authors of the studies incorporated in your literature review, you will not be able to critique the study with any confidence. It is therefore advisable that once you are aware of the predominant research methods that have been used by researchers studying your particular area, that you develop your understanding of these methods before you begin to critique the studies. For example, if you have identified many randomised controlled trials (RCTs), you are strongly advised to read about the method of undertaking RCTs before you commence your critical appraisal. Clearly this is harder if your literature search leads you to a wide cross-section of research methods. You are not expected to develop an in-depth under-standing of every research approach in the way that you would be able to if you had identified papers using just one or two approaches. You are advised to discuss this when writing the limitations of your study in the methods section of your literature review.

The Critical Appraisal Skills Programme (CASP)

One set of critical appraisal tools suitable for those new to the process are produced by The Critical Appraisal Skills Programme (CASP), developed by the Oxford University Public Health Resources Unit. The advantage of the CASP critical appraisal tool is that there is a specific critical appraisal tool for most, if not all, of the studies you are likely to encounter. CASP have published critical appraisal tools for review articles, qualitative studies, RCTs, cohort and case control studies. They are easily available on the internet. At undergraduate level, you are advised to consider the ten main questions only and not to consider the additional more detailed questions. Those studying at postgraduate level might want to refer to these more detailed questions.

Writing your critical appraisal of each paper

Whichever critical appraisal tool you use, you will need to appraise each of the papers that you have identified that address your research ques-tion. You do not need to include a completed detailed critical appraisal of each paper in your final review, but you will need to demonstrate how you undertook the critical appraisal. As a general rule, at undergraduate level, you would expect to include a paragraph summarising your critical appraisal of each paper you reviewed. This will be more extensive at postgraduate level. You should include this the *first* time you refer to the paper when you write up your results. Subsequently, you do not need to include this critical appraisal summary each time you refer back to this paper. It is then helpful to include a copy of the critical appraisal tools you use in the appendix of your review.

Some approaches to critical appraisal of the following types of literature will be considered:

- review articles
- quantitative studies
- qualitative studies
- non-research information, for example articles that convey the author's point of view or anecdotal evidence.

Critical appraisal of review articles

The first step in the critical appraisal of a review article is to determine whether or not the review has been undertaken **systematically**. The amount of detail given to the search, critiquing and bringing together of the evidence will differ with each literature review that has attempted to incorporate a systematic approach. The review may be described as a Cochrane Collaboration review, in which case you can be fairly confident that it is a review that has been undertaken systematically. However, the main way to determine whether a review has been approached systematically is to scrutinise the methods used to conduct the review. Readers can then determine whether the reviewers undertook a Cochrane-style systematic review or a less detailed, but none the less systematic approach to the review. For example, a Cochrane-style systematic review aims to uncover all literature on the topic in question, whereas a less detailed review acknowledges that the search will not be comprehensive but will identify which databases were searched. Furthermore, while a Cochrane-style systematic review will have a team of researchers who work together in the critical analysis of the literature, a less detailed review is likely to be carried out by a single researcher with fewer resources for collaboration in these aspects. Those undertaking a systematic approach to reviewing the literature should ensure that they are explicit about the methods used to achieve this review and to demonstrate that they did everything in their power to ensure their approach was as systematic as possible.

Throughout this book, the rationale and process of undertaking a literature review in a systematic manner has been discussed. Those undertaking a literature review will therefore be familiar with this research method and this will assist them in determining the strengths and limitations of the reviews they encounter. Authors of a review that has been approached systematically would be expected to incorporate discussion of the search strategy, method of critical appraisal and comparison of the literature, as outlined in this book.

These principles are largely incorporated into the tools that are available for the critical appraisal of review articles. One of the critical appraisal tools for the appraisal of a systematic review is the CASP tool (see above). This was developed by the Public Health Research Unit at the University of Oxford and can be found at the following link: www.phru.nhs.uk/casp/casp.htm. Key questions in the CASP tool include whether the review asks a clearly focused question and also includes appropriate literature to address the question, then whether the review attempted to include all the studies and whether these were appraised and appropriately brought together. Crombie (2006) discusses the critical appraisal of review papers and suggests that those undertaking a critical appraisal of a review should consider the following essential questions: How were the papers identified? How was the quality of the papers assessed? and How were the results summarised?

Those reviewing review articles should be able to determine whether the review was undertaken in an explicitly systematic way or whether a more narrative approach has been used. This will determine the quality of evidence that the review provides. A review incorporating a systematic approach will present stronger evidence than a review in which the method is not explicit. The strengths and limitations of the review should be documented when the review is discussed within the context of the literature review.

Dealing with existing literature reviews

Those undertaking a literature review are often unsure how they should proceed if they identify a systematic review in the same topic area as their own literature review. Critical appraisal of the review is clearly vital here. The worst case scenario is that a student encounters a recently published systematic review in the literature whose focus is the same as their own literature review. The first step is to assess the quality of the review, to determine whether it is a systematic review or more of a narrative review. If there is no explicitly recorded method of how the literature was searched, critiqued and analysed, then the quality of the review may not be easy to determine. It may therefore be appropriate to proceed with a systematic approach to the literature review.

If critical appraisal of the systematic review identifies a good quality review and this is encountered early on in your course of study, it would be wise to alter the question slightly so as to avoid direct repetition of the review question. You could be penalised for lack of originality and it could be difficult to demonstrate that the review was undertaken in a thorough and independent way without relying on ideas that were found already published in another review. However, if the systematic review is identified once you are already immersed in the literature review process and a change of question is not desirable, this should be fully documented in the methods section of your literature review. You should then make an extra effort to ensure that the originality of your work is established and that the methods of search, critiquing and analysing the literature are clearly documented so that it is clear that the results you present are your own work.

If a systematic review is encountered that is a direct repetition of your review question, but was published a few years previously, you can use this review as the background to your own review and focus your own review on providing an update to the review that already exists. The search strategy you undertake can reflect this, with your search strategy commencing at the point at which the original systematic review ceased to search for literature. This can be established from the method of the established systematic review. With reduced time span over which to search, you will have more time to search wider and deeper for harder to access materials. This will improve the quality of your literature review.

When a systematic review is encountered that addresses in part the research question but is not a direct replication of the question, the systematic review should be critically appraised and incorporated into your literature review. If you are undertaking a review of the literature you will already have knowledge of the research method, which you can draw on when you critique reviews that you encounter. You can then apply this knowledge to the systematic review you have identified with the use of a critical appraisal tool relevant to the review of systematic review. You can then consider the relevance of the review to your research question.

Critical appraisal of quantitative studies

Most quantitative studies that you will encounter fall into one of the following categories: randomised controlled trial (or similar trial), case control study, cohort study or cross-sectional study using questionnaire/surveys. One of the main approaches to assessing the quality of quantitative work is to assess the validity and reliability of the study. Validity refers to whether the study measures what it intends to measure, and reliability refers to whether the measurement is reliable and would yield the same results on repeated measurements. There are CASP critical appraisal tools for randomised controlled trials, cohort studies and case control trials. These can be located at: www.phru.nhs.uk/casp/casp.htm.

Your critical appraisal of quantitative studies will be greatly assisted if you are familiar with the particular research method used in the study. This can be difficult for those who encounter a wide range of literature, as a novice researcher cannot be expected to have in-depth knowledge of all research methods. However, those who find that their search strategy leads them to papers incorporating one or two research methods are advised to develop their understanding of these particular methods. In order to assist your understanding of each study that you have identified, the following questions can be asked of each quantitative paper.

What is the journal of publication?

Those reviewing quantitative research should be aware of the quality of the journal in which the research is published. In principle, a journal is considered to be of good quality if it is peer reviewed – that is, each paper is reviewed by at least one recognised expert in the subject area about which the paper is written, prior to acceptance for publication in the journal. However, it should be noted that the peer review process is not perfect. Papers are generally considered by one or two experts in a field and it is not possible for an expert to know every aspect about any particular topic. It is not uncommon for corrections or amendments to a paper to appear in later publications of the journal. In reality, the peer review process takes place when the research paper is published!

What is the research question and why was the study conducted?

The study question should be clear and should be founded on argument and rationale as to why the study was undertaken.

What method was selected to undertake the research?

In most papers there will be a short summary of the research process undertaken and from this you will be able to identify how the study was conducted.

How big was the sample?

The sample refers to those who took part in the study. The sample will be taken from the wider population to whom the research project relates. For example, a sample of university students could be taken from the university population as a whole. Sample size in quantitative research tends to be large. This is because researchers are concerned with validity: that is, whether the findings of a study are valid or reflect reality. For example, you are likely to have greater confidence in a study comparing two treatment options in which many thousands of people had participated than a study conducted on just 20 participants. However, if the condition under investigation is unusual, sample sizes inevitably will be smaller. The authors of quantitative research papers should demonstrate how they determined the sample size for the research in question. This should be clearly documented in the paper and is often referred to as a power calculation.

Has the appropriate sample been obtained?

You need to question who was selected to participate in the study. Quantitative research sometimes uses **random sampling**. This means that the sample is picked at random from the overall population. Random sampling is generally defined as meaning that all those in the sample have an equal chance of being selected in the sample. This is important because it ensures that the sample is not biased. For example, a random sample of university students could be drawn from the university admission lists rather than from the attendance at lectures, given that all students will be on the admission list, but not all will attend lectures. Any sample drawn from those who attend lectures will be biased rather than random. It is important to note that obtaining an unbiased sample in any research study is very difficult. A questionnaire might be sent to a random sample of the population, but unless there is a 100 per cent response rate, the responses obtained will be biased. It is also important to note that some studies use random allocation within a non-random sample, rather than random sampling overall. A randomised controlled trial, for example, will normally have a convenience sample from which two or three random groups are composed. When you are reviewing a quantitative study, be aware of the sampling strategy and be able to comment on the reasons as to why this approach has been adopted. Consider whether a random or non-random sample was used and whether this was appropriate.

How were the data collected?

The data collection method should be appropriate for the study design. Quantitative research often uses a wide variety of data collection methods for attributes that are appropriate for objective measurement.

How were the data analysed?

Quantitative data are usually analysed statistically and students should expect to find reference to the statistical tests used in the paper in order to make sense of the data. There are two types of statistics.

First of all there are **descriptive statistics** that describe the data given in the paper. These statistics should describe clearly the main results: for example, how many people answered 'yes' to a particular question, or what the most common response to a question was. The average answers will typically be given using the mean, median and mode responses. The data should be clearly described so that you can identify the main findings of the paper.

Secondly, there are **inferential statistics**. The purpose of inferential statistics is to **generalise** to the wider population. In other words, to determine the extent to which the data obtained from a sample are representative of the wider population as a whole. Inferential statistics provide a means of drawing conclusions about a population, using the data obtained from a sample taken from that population. For example, if you have a questionnaire survey of 1000 people, of which 500 stated a preference for holidaying abroad, inferential statistics can be used to determine whether this result would be accurate for the whole population, rather than this sample. Inferential statistics do more than describe a sample, they infer from it to the wider population. The bigger the sample, the surer you can be that the sample prevalence is close to the population prevalence. The confidence we can have that the sample is an accurate indication of the true population prevalence is reflected in **confidence intervals**, which give numerical limits to a 'common sense' approach. Confidence intervals are used to estimate the confidence that the sample reflects a range within which the true score is known to lie. The smaller the interval or range, the more confident you can be that the results in the study reflect the results you would find in the larger population. Using a formula, the confidence intervals, upper and lower are calculated. A 95 per cent confidence interval means that we can be 95 per cent sure that the true population prevalence lies between the lower and upper confidence interval.

Example: 100 students are asked to document the number of hours per week spent using a mobile phone. The mean number of hours is 4. The confidence intervals are calculated as 2.5–5.6. This means that you can be 95 per cent confident that students spend between 2.5 and 5.6 hours per week using a mobile phone.

Statistics are often described as a **p value** or probability value. The p value expresses the probability of the results shown in the paper being due to chance. P values test a hypothesis. They remove the 'best guess' that the results found are not due to chance. It is important to determine the play of chance in any research. Let's say you are undertaking a randomised controlled trial and have two randomly allocated groups A and B. Normally in a RCT, you would give an intervention to one group and not to the other and then examine the differences in outcomes between the groups. However, let's say that on one occasion no intervention was given. Both groups were treated with the standard treatment. Yet when you examine the outcomes in each group, you will inevitably see a variety of outcomes in each group, due to natural differences between the groups, even though both groups were given the same treatment. Now let's say that you do then administer an intervention to one of the groups and observe the different outcomes of the two groups. The p value can then be calculated to determine whether the differences in outcomes observed is due to chance. To calculate the P value we use the **null hypothesis**. The null hypothesis states that there is no relationship between the variables under study. The p value expresses the probability of the results occurring, if the null hypothesis were true; that is if no relationship was found. This can be calculated using a statistical test, for example the Chi squared test. A p value of 0.05, for example, means 0.05 (1:20) chance of seeing these results if the null hypothesis were true. This means it is unlikely that the null hypothesis is true and that there is a relationship between the variables. It is important to remember that this does not indicate a causal relationship, that is that one variable caused the other, but just that the two occur together.

Example: Take the following hypothesis: Students who get a 2:1 degree are more likely to enter clinical management than those who get a 2:2. The null hypothesis is that there is no difference in degree outcome in those entering management. In a study of 100 students, 30 students obtained a 2:1 and entered management, 20 students obtained a 2:2 and entered management. The Chi square test showed a P value of 0.2 which means that there is a one in five chance that these results were due to chance rather than the effect of degree classification.

Additional resources for critical appraisal

In addition to the specific CASP appraisal tools, there are further resources for those reviewing quantitative studies. Those reviewing randomised controlled trials, are advised to refer to the **CONSORT statement**. The CONSORT (Consolidated Standards of Reporting Trials) statement was issued in 1996 and revised in 2001. The CONSORT statement was issued in response to concern about the quality of the reporting of randomised controlled trials submitted for publication. There was concern that without thorough and transparent reporting of the process of conducting the RCT, the quality of the trials could not be assessed. The CONSORT statement comprises a checklist and flow diagram to enable both the researchers and those reviewing the research to identify good practice in the conduct and presentation of RCTs. The aim of the CONSORT statement is to make the process of undertaking and publishing RCTs as clear as possible, so that users of the research can evaluate the strengths and limitations of the study. The CONSORT statement gives clear guidance to researchers concerning which aspects of the design of the RCT they should make explicit to readers of the research, to ensure that those who read and use the research have clear information concerning the way in which the RCT was conducted. Full details of the revised CONSORT statement are given by Moher *et al.* (2001). The statement includes discussion of the scientific background for the study, eligibility of participants and interventions intended for each group, random allocation and blinding, statistical analysis and discussion of results.

For those reviewing cohort studies Rochon *et al.* (2005) have identified factors to consider when considering the quality of the studies. These can be used in conjunction with the CASP critical appraisal tool for cohort studies. Rochon *et al.* recommend that the following aspects of the trial are taken into consideration. Firstly, the comparison made between the groups is observed. This includes how the groups were selected and how they were defined. Secondly, whether the comparison makes sense is considered, in other words whether a cohort study was a useful method of studying the research topic. Thirdly, consideration of the potential selection biases is made. The important difference between an RCT and a cohort study is that in an RCT there are two or more groups that are allocated at random. Each group receives different treatment and the differences in outcome can be attributed to the treatment given, as the groups were allocated at random and therefore considered equal in all respects other than the treatment given. In a cohort study, the cohort and control group are not allocated at random but arise naturally in the population. For example, those who use illicit drugs might be a naturally occurring cohort group. This group of illicit drug users can then be compared with non-users at the end of the trial. Any differences between the two groups cannot be attributed to the exposure or intervention given, as the cohort and control groups were never equal.

For those reviewing cross-sectional studies, Crombie (2006) suggests that the following essential questions are asked of case control studies. How were the cases obtained? Was the control group appropriate? Was data collected in the same way for cases as for controls?

For those reviewing surveys/questionnaires, at the time of writing this book, there is a lack of formal appraisal tools or checklists to assist with the process of critical appraisal. There are, however, texts that give thorough information and advice about the construction of questionnaires and surveys, for example Oppenheim's (1992) classic text entitled *Questionnaire design and attitude measurement*. If you have many questionnaire survey studies to appraise, you are well advised to become familiar with these principles of questionnaire design.

Boynton and Greenhalgh (2004) comment on the ease with which questionnaires are distributed without due regard to the process of ensuring that the questionnaire will facilitate the collection of useful data. They discuss the frequent use of poorly designed questionnaires that lack rigour and hence lead to the collection of poor quality data and subsequently to misleading conclusions. Boynton and Greenhalgh (2004 p. 1312) assert 'No single method has been so abused'. They also warn that elementary errors in carrying out questionnaire/survey research are common and suggest the following questions to appraise the studies.

What information is required and whether a questionnaire is appropriate

For a questionnaire to be useful, researchers must know in advance what questions they need to ask. If very little is known about a particular area, further exploratory work may need to be done prior to the development of the questionnaire.

Whether there is an existing instrument and whether this has been tested for validity and reliability

A questionnaire will only collect useful data if the questions have been well tested and piloted. This is to ensure that the questions mean the same thing to those who respond as they do to those who designed them. This will also include how the questions are presented.

How the sample is selected

Even with the best designed questionnaire, unless it is distributed to a representative sample of the population, the quality of the results will be reduced. A postal questionnaire can be distributed to a random sample of the population; however, it is highly unlikely that everyone will respond. This affects the quality of the data as it is not known how the responses from those who did not respond would have differed from those who did. Alternatively, if it is possible to distribute a questionnaire face-to-face, you may achieve a higher response rate, but you will not achieve a random sample, as you are only selecting participants from those patients/clients attending on a particular day. For example, if you distributed the questionnaire in a shopping centre on a Saturday, you would reach a different population than if the questionnaire was distributed on a weekday. Similarly, you would be likely to get a different group of people depending on the time at which the questionnaire was distributed. Thus, it is very difficult to achieve a random sample in a questionnaire survey which is distributed face-to-face as only those in attendance on that day have the possibility to respond to a questionnaire. It is equally very difficult to achieve a random sample in a postal questionnaire as the response rates tend to be low. For these reasons and due to the difficulty of creating a questionnaire that measures what you intend to measure, the quality of data obtained from questionnaires will be affected by the methods used and needs to be carefully considered in each case.

In summary, for those critiquing quantitative research, there are two main objectives. Firstly, you should become as familiar as possible with the research approach undertaken in the study. Secondly, you should apply this knowledge when reviewing the rigour of the study with the use of an appropriate critical appraisal tool.

Critical appraisal of qualitative studies

There has been much discussion in recent years concerning the ways in which qualitative research is evaluated and this debate is ongoing. With the advent of evidence-based practice and the need to demonstrate accountability in research, there has been increasing demand for evidence of rigour in qualitative research. Clearly without evidence of rigour in the undertaking of the study, the worth of any study can be questioned. However, the search for evidence of rigour in qualitative research is difficult due to the interpretative and exploratory nature of qualitative studies. It can therefore be difficult for those who critique a qualitative study to determine the strengths and limitations of the study. This is because qualitative studies typically do not seek to quantify or measure the items under exploration using numbers – an approach which lies traditionally in the quantitative domain, in which the measurements taken by the researchers are repeatable and re-testable. In contrast, most qualitative studies use exploratory interviews, focus groups or observations in order to collect a rich data set which can then be analysed qualitatively, that is by exploring emerging themes rather than by statistics. The aim of most qualitative data analysis is to study the interview scripts or other data obtained for the study and to develop an understanding of this data. The data are coded and themes are then generated from the data set. The generation of themes, although rigorous, is interpretative and subjective, depending on the insight of the researcher. Qualitative data analysis is therefore open to interpretation. Because the researcher is involved in, and indeed shapes, both the data collection and analysis process, it is not possible for the researcher to remain detatched from the data which are collected. It is also not desirable to strive for this detatchment. The richness of qualitative enquiry arises from the dialogue between the researcher and the researched, and the insights obtained through this process are only possible because of the interaction between the two. For example, the interviewer may probe the interviewee about his or her responses to a question and so phrases the next question as a direct response to the reply received. The richness of the data is dependent on the interaction between the researcher and researched and the process is necessarily subjective. Subjectivity is required for the researcher to get an insight into the topic of investigation and objectivity is not strived for. The concept of reflexivity refers to the acknowledgement by the qualitative researcher that the process of enquiry is necessarily open to interpretation and that detatchment from the focus of the research is neither desirable or possible. Guba and Lincoln (1995) reinforce this argument by describing the construction of the findings of qualitative research – constructed by the dialogue between the researcher and the researched.

How should we critique qualitative research?

For the reasons outlined, there has been much debate about how the strengths and limitations of a qualitative study can be determined. Concern has been expressed about qualitative research being subject to the same criteria for reliability and validity as quantitative studies (Horsburgh 2003). Horsburgh argues that if qualitative research is judged by the same standard as quantitative research, then the impression may be created that qualitative research is not academically rigorous. Yet, qualitative researchers adhere to procedures that ensure rigour throughout the research process.

As discussed in an earlier section, the quality of quantitative work is often assessed for the validity and reliability of the study. Because the 'measurements' obtained in qualitative research are made through the interpretation of the researchers, most qualitative researchers argue that it is not possible to assess qualitative research in the same way as quantitative research. For this reason. Lincoln and Guba (1985) argue that the terms credibility, transferability, dependability, and confirmability are more appropriate to assessing the quality of a qualitative study than terms such as validity and reliability. They argue that all qualitative research should have a 'truth value' and that this could be determined by strategies that represent the hallmark of good qualitative research, such as keeping an accurate trail of the research process and transparency in the data analysis process.

Yet despite concern about the appropriate way to assess the quality of qualitative research, not all researchers agree with Lincoln and Guba's approach to the assessment of quality in qualitative research. Morse *et al.* (2002) argue that the approach advocated by Lincoln and Guba is unhelpful as it encourages researchers to review the quality of the research at the end of the research process rather than to keep re-evaluating the quality of the research process as the research is ongoing. Morse argues that the terms validity and reliability are appropriate to qualitative research and cites Kvale (1989) who argues that validity means to investigate, to check and to question – all of which are necessary components of any quality assessment of qualitative research.

It is important for those who review qualitative research to be aware that there is no consensus among qualitative researchers about what constitutes a good qualitative study, how a study is critiqued or the terminology to be used when referring to both qualitative studies and critiquing tools (Popay *et al.* 1998, Sandelowski and Barrosso 2002, Russell and Gregory 2003). Consequently, you are likely to encounter a variety of qualitative research incorporating a wide range of approaches and methods, and an equally wide variety of appraisal tools for the critique of qualitative research. You need to be aware of these tensions so that you are not confused by the different approaches and rationale when these are encountered. It is also important that you are familiar with the basic principles of qualitative research and how the approach differs from quantitative research, so that you can assess the individual quality of the research you encounter.

Critical appraisal tools for qualitative studies

The diverse nature of qualitative research means that it is often difficult to critique, especially for a novice researcher. It is also argued that it is difficult to find an appraisal tool within qualitative research that is appropriate for every qualitative research paper encountered. Barbour (2001) argues that the vast diversity of qualitative methods means that the critique of any qualitative paper by means of a simple checklist or appraisal tool can be difficult. However, the benefits of using a critical appraisal tool rather than using an unstructured approach have also been highlighted. You are therefore advised to use a tool when appraising qualitative research but to be aware of the limitations of doing so and also to be aware that the tool may not be appropriate for every such piece of research.

There are a variety of critical appraisal tools available and an internet search will enable you to view many of those accessible. As outlined above, because of the complexity of the topic, there is no one tool that is best for all qualitative research; however one of the commonly used appraisal tools is the CASP qualitative critical appraisal tool, available at www.phru.nhs.uk/casp/casp.htm It should be noted that at under-graduate level, students using the CASP tool are advised to address the headings that are in bold text only and not to attend to the detail that is required in the additional questions which are found in the subheadings. Other useful resources for students are the guide to critiquing qualitative studies found in the research methods textbook by Polit and Beck (2005) and the paper by Greenhalgh and Taylor (1997).

You are advised to use a critical appraisal tool – rather than no tool at all – and whichever tool is selected, it is very important that you are familiar with the general principles of qualitative research, as outlined in Chapter 2, so that you can apply the appraisal tool appropriately to any given study. Some general principles to assist with the critical appraisal are given below.

Who wrote the paper?

In qualitative research it is particularly important that the researchers have the necessary experience to undertake the research. This is because in qualitative research the quality of the data that are collected is depen-dent on the skills of the researcher. Qualitative research is reflexive, which means that the researcher's own values, experience and interests shape the research process. The researcher interacts with the participants in order to get as much insight into the research topic as possible and, therefore, the best quality data. The researcher may ask probing ques-tions to get richer data on a particular aspect of the topic and the way that this is done reflects the experience and expertise of the researcher. Therefore, questions that can be asked of the author include their rele-vant qualifications and experience and whether they have the necessary insight into the topic area to address the research question.

Where is the paper published?

Those reviewing qualitative research need to be aware of the accredited quality of the journal in which the research is published. As mentioned previously, you should consider whether the journal is peer reviewed.

Is there a research question and is the method appropriate for addressing the question?

Qualitative research will commence with an identified research question and the method chosen to address the question should be appropriate to this. For example, if the research question is exploratory, for example:

'How do people who are homeless describe their experience living in a hostel?', then the method of answering the question should also be explorative, as is appropriate for qualitative study. In the second chapter of this book, a brief introduction to the different approaches to qualitative research were outlined. Those reviewing qualitative research should be familiar with the different approaches so that they can identify why a particular approach has been adopted in any research study. For example, researchers who are interested in exploring participants' experience of being homeless might adopt a phenomenological approach to their research. However, a phenomenological approach would not be appropriate for those interested in exploring the attitudes of those who are homeless as this type of study is concerned with exploring the lived experience only, rather than attitudes related to this. An appropriate approach to exploring the lived experience of people who are homeless might be to interview people who have had this experience. It would not be appropriate to observe people who are homeless as this would not achieve an insight into the way in which they would describe their experience. Thus, it is important that the method chosen to address the question is appropriate to the research question itself.

Was the right qualitative research method used?

The selected data collection method should also be appropriate to the method and research question. The most commonly used data collection methods in qualitative research are in-depth interviews, focus groups and observation. Those reviewing qualitative research reports should assess how the data collection methods were determined and the appropriateness of these to the research question. In-depth interviews are used when the insight into a particular topic is sought from the participant. The interviewer will be trained and skilled in asking questions that probe into the experience of the participant and the aim is to generate rich data through one-to-one dialogue. Focus groups are a form of group interview and may be selected over in-depth interviews when dialogue between research participants – rather than in-depth discussion with one participant – is regarded as a positive contribution to the study. For example, if the research topic is unfamiliar to those involved and participants may not have developed their thoughts in relation to this topic, focus groups can be useful as a data collection method as the ideas expressed by one participant may trigger a response in another participant. However, if a topic is particularly sensitive, participants may be reluctant to express their thoughts in a focus group and in-depth interviews may be more appropriate.

The role of questionnaires in the collection of qualitative data should be mentioned at this point. While it is possible to collect qualitative data though open-ended questions on a questionnaire schedule, such data are not likely to be as in-depth as that collected through one-to-one interaction. Therefore, when a qualitative research study incorporates a questionnaire survey into its methods, the quality of the qualitative data collected should be considered carefully. Data collected through observation is especially useful when actual observations are sought rather than participants' interpretations. For example, the extent to which nurses comply with infection control policies can be measured more accurately through direct observation than any other method, as it is well known that participants may not accurately self-report their behaviour. It is important to note that observational data may be used in both quantitative and qualitative studies. For example, the number of infection control practices undertaken by each practitioner could be counted numerically, or the nature of the interaction between practitioner and patient could be observed using qualitative approaches. Therefore, when reviewing a qualitative study, you should make an assessment as to the appropriateness of the chosen method used in the study in addressing the research question.

What was the sample for the study?

Most qualitative researchers use purposive sampling rather than random sampling in their research. It is important to be aware of the differences between the two. A random sample is where participants are picked at random from the population being studied and every person in that population has an equal chance of being selected. For example, a random sample of students could be identified from the college records with every fifth student being selected. In purposive sampling, an appropriate sample from the population is chosen according to particular criteria. Participants are chosen for their suitability to provide rich data for in-depth study. For this reason, random sampling would be inappropriate as it may fail to identify information-rich participants. Thus any qualitative study that uses random sampling rather than purposive sampling should cause you to question why this particular approach was adopted. You should also consider the type of participant who makes up the purposive sample. For example, if the researchers are exploring people who are homeless, then a purposive sample obtained in Glasgow is likely to be very different to a sample from London. Similarly, the characteristics of a sample are likely to vary depending on the particular area in Glasgow from which the sample is drawn. This will affect the extent to which the results are transferable from one context to another and, therefore, the relevance of the particular research study to the literature review question. An alternative sampling strategy that might be used in qualitative research is theoretical sampling. Theoretical sampling is an approach commonly used in grounded theory in which the sample is identified as the study progresses, according to the needs of the study. Another sampling strategy is snowball sampling, in which the sample is developed as new potential participants are identified as the study progresses. For example, the contacts of participants already involved in the research may be invited to enter the study, if they have the relevant experience. You would expect to find that purposive, theoretical or snowball sampling are used in a qualitative study.

How big was the sample?

Sample size in qualitative research tends to be small. The sample should be large enough to achieve sufficient information-rich cases for in-depth data analysis, but not so large that the amount of data obtained becomes unmanageable. A small sample is required because in-depth understanding (rather than statistical analysis) is sought from information-rich participants who take part. For this reason, a small sample size should be regarded as appropriate in qualitative research. This is in contrast to quantitative research in which the nearer the sample size is to the true population, the more representative the results will be. Russell and Gregory (2003) argue that different qualitative approaches require different sample sizes and advise that phenomenological studies tend to have smaller samples than grounded theory studies or ethnographic studies. When you are reviewing a study it is important to consider the account given by the researchers of the way in which the sample size was arrived at throughout the course of any study.

How were the data collected?

The way in which the data were collected should also be considered. Most researchers advocate that in-depth interviews and focus groups should be tape-recorded so that the interviews can be transcribed word for word. However, some researchers argue that this is time-consuming and that the time could be better used by undertaking additional interviews and hence collecting considerably more data. There are many variations in the way that qualitative data may be collected. For example, some researchers advocate that interview transcripts are returned to the participants in order that the participants check and validate the content of the transcript for accuracy. However, other researchers argue that this is time-consuming and unnecessarily burdensome on participants who may not remember the interview or who may not wish to revisit the content of the interview they gave (Barbour 2001). They may also wish to alter the content of the interview, thus affecting its validity. It is important that the researchers justify the approach they have taken to the data collection process and can demonstrate that the process was undertaken systematically and rigorously.

How were the data analysed?

The reviewer should consider the way in which the method of data analysis is reported in a qualitative research study. Although word restrictions impose limitations on the detail that can be given in any journal paper, there should be evidence of a considered approach to data analysis. Use of a computer package may be evident, but this in itself does not ensure rigour in the analysis process. Equally it is possible to demonstrate rigour in data analysis without the use of computer packages. There should also be justification as to how much data had been collected and whether saturation was achieved. The concept of data saturation might be discussed in the study. Data saturation means that at the end of the analysis period, the continuing data analysis does not identify additional new themes from the data, but instead the data that is analysed merely adds to the existing themes that have emerged from previous data analysis.

In summary, critical appraisal of qualitative research papers is complex and while novice researchers are expected to be aware of the complexities and many different approaches to undertaking qualitative studies, they are not expected to offer a contribution to the debate. Those reviewing qualitative research should become familiar with the particular approaches to qualitative study that have been used in the papers they have identified. They should then assess the rigour of the papers with the aid of a critical appraisal tool.

Critical appraisal of other sources of information

There is likely to be much published information relating to your topic that is not the report of empirical research. This information can be incorporated usefully into your review and contribute to addressing your research question. This information might be used to add context to your introduction and discussion chapters, especially when the results of empirical studies conflict. However, it is important that all information is critically appraised for the quality of evidence it provides. Evidence from non-empirical research is usually anecdotal evidence only. In terms of the hierarchy of evidence, non-research articles are described as a weak form of evidence and, at best, expert opinion.

An approach to evaluating discussion articles

Those using non-research based evidence in their literature review need to identify how they are going to assess the quality of this information, in the same way as they would consider the quality of primary research or systematic review. For example, a discussion article written by a leading expert in a particular area might be considered to carry more weight than a similar article written by a student. Hek *et al.* (2000) report the following criteria for critiquing non-research articles:

- Is the subject relevant to the review question?
- Is it accurate?
- Is it well written and credible?
- Is it peer reviewed in any way?
- Does it ring true?
- In what quality of journal is the report published?

Reviewers are also encouraged to examine the following attributes of a paper to determine the quality of the information provided: the intended target audience, credentials of the author, the publisher of the information, and the way in which the information is presented. That is to say, the extent to which the author is suitably qualified to report on the topic in question should be examined. Similarly, an article would carry more weight if it was published in an academic journal rather than in a newspaper. However, it is important to remember that the expert opinion of a well known figure in the area might be found to contradict established findings from empirical research. For example, in recent discussions about climate change, many experts have been consulted about their perception of current signs of climate change. However, in the absence of empirical evidence, the validity of their opinion can only be speculated. It should be noted that information obtained from websites can be critically appraised using this approach.

An approach to evaluating the quality of a written argument

Another approach to reviewing the quality of a non-empirical research paper in which arguments are presented, is to assess the quality of the arguments presented in the paper. This approach was originally advocated by Thouless and Thouless (1953), who discuss the use of logic in the constructed argument presented in a discussion paper. They articulate 38 'dishonest tricks' commonly used in argument, for example:

- using emotionally charged words
- making statements using words such as 'all' when 'some' would be more appropriate
- using selected instances
- misrepresentation of opposing arguments
- evasion of a sound refutation of an argument.

You are also advised to consult the 15 item checklist devised by Cottrell (2005) for the evaluation of an academic essay. Criteria include whether the conclusion is clear and based on evidence, whether the arguments are well structured and presented in a logical order, whether good use is made of alternative arguments and whether these are referenced.

Those reviewing discussion articles and expert opinions are encouraged to scrutinise the way in which the article is written as a guide to the strength of argument presented. Reviewers should question the use of language, the acknowledgement of alternative approaches or lines of argument, forced analogy, false credentials, and so on. Does the evidence on which the arguments are founded bear scrutiny? If the arguments are well constructed and defensible, then greater weight can be given to these arguments over those that are less well prepared and constructed. Consider George Monbiot's response to David Bellamy in the *Guardian* (2005) regarding the evidence behind the environmental threat presented by global warming. George Monbiot refers to recent research findings to reinforce his argument while David Bellamy argues from his opinion only. If you applied Thouless and Thouless' (1953) criteria to these arguments, which one would have greater credibility?

An approach to evaluating information contained on websites

There can be no doubt that the internet contains a wealth of information that may be useful for health and social care practitioners. Indeed, there is even evidence that internet searches can be used by health and social care for the benefit of their patients and clients (Giustini 2005, Tang and Hwee Kwoon Ng 2006). However, it has to be acknowledged that websites are unregulated and it is possible for anybody to publish anything on an internet site. You are therefore recommended to be critical of any websites you encounter. Fink (2005) suggests that you should ask the following questions of any websites you encounter:

- Who supports the site?
- When was it last updated?
- What authority do the authors of the site have?

If you are happy with the answers you get to these questions, any material you encounter on a website can be subjected to the critical appraisal strategies as advocated by Hek *et al.* (2000), Thouless and Thouless (1953) and Cotterell (2005).

While it is possible and necessary to critique the quality of non-research information incorporated into a review, it is important for the reviewer to remember that non-research articles do not usually represent strong evidence upon which to draw conclusions. Non-research articles should be appraised using the guidelines suggested above and incorporated into the study, whilst acknowledging the limitations inherent in the evidence they give.

Tips for writing up your critique of the literature

1 Remember that to critique means to give the positive and negative points about a paper. You are not expected only to be critical. Emphasise the good points about the paper.
2 Remember that no research paper is perfect!
3 Remember to describe the critical appraisal tools you use. Be explicit

about the way you appraised the information, including non-research papers.

4 Remember to give a summary of your critical appraisal of each paper the *first* time you refer to it.

5 You will not have time to debate the strengths and limitations of any research paper in great detail. One paragraph per paper is about right.

6 You need to be able to summarise what the aims of the paper are, what the authors did, what the results showed and, finally, your review of the quality of the paper.

In summary

At this stage in your literature review, you should be able to discuss with confidence the relevance and strengths and limitations of your literature to your research question. As a general rule, you do not need an extensive discussion of the qualities of each paper but you should be able to summarise the main points. When you come to write up your results, you should not mention any paper without discussing the type and the quality of evidence that this paper provides. A few sentences or a short paragraph will normally be sufficient for each paper. The purpose of critical appraisal is to determine the relevance, strengths and limitations of the information collected so that you can determine the weight each paper should have in answering the research question. A study might be well carried out but not specific enough to address your research question. Alternatively, a study might be very relevant to your research question but not well designed or implemented. Furthermore, non-empirical information might add interesting insight to your argument, but the quality of this information also needs to be assessed. Without this critical appraisal, the contribution of this evidence to addressing the research question cannot be assessed. The controversy surrounding the MMR vaccination, outlined earlier, illustrates this point only too well. The final stage of your literature review is to combine the evidence and present your findings. This is addressed in the next chapter.

Key points

1 Critical appraisal is a necessary process in determining the relevance and quality of the published information related to your research question.
2 You need to read and re-read your papers before you can begin to appraise critically.
3 You need to distinguish between papers that report empirical findings and those that present discussion or expert opinion only.
4 You are advised to use one of the many critical appraisal tools that are available to structure your critical appraisal.

6

How do I synthesise my findings?

Combining the evidence • Three 'advanced' approaches for summing up the literature • Meta-analysis • Meta-ethnography • Meta-study • A simplified approach • Providing a summary of your information • Comparing and contrasting the results of each study • Working with codes and themes that do not support each other • Discussion of the strength of evidence • Be aware of results that appear too neat • Be creative! • Writing up your results • Telling a story with your data • Incorporating your critical appraisal • What do I do if my information only partially addresses my research question? • Tips for writing up your synthesis of the literature • In summary • Key points

By the time you have reached this stage, you have already come a long way. You will have identified a research question, devised an appropriate search strategy to identify information that will answer your question, and read and critically appraised this information to assess the strengths and limitations of the evidence you have found. You are coming towards the end of your study; however, it is important not to lose momentum at this stage.

Combining the evidence

By now, you will be familiar with the results of all of the studies and have completed a critical appraisal for each of the papers you have. You are ready for the next stage of your literature review – to bring these together so that you can address your research question. The aim of this process is to **summarise** the findings of your literature review into manageable amounts. However, you are aiming to achieve more than just a summary of your results. The aim is to **interpret** the results. This will allow you to consider why one study obtained a different set of results to that obtained by a similar study, and how the results of each study were shaped by the methods used to collect the data. You are seeking to explain the differences and similarities in the different papers that you have, rather than to simply summarise them.

According to Fingeld (2003 p. 894), the goal is to 'produce a new and integrative interpretation of findings that is more substantive than those resulting from individual investigation'. The aim is to bring together the different studies or other pieces of information and to find new meaning from the sum of these papers viewed as a whole than could be obtained by reading each one individually.

This might seem a daunting task, but if it is tackled in a step-by-step manner as this chapter will illustrate, it will become manageable. Importantly, it is this process that makes your literature review original and unique. The discoveries and insights you make as you compare and contrast the literature are only possible because you have followed the systematic process of identifying and reviewing the published information relating to your topic. They are testament to your developing skills as a researcher.

One common term for this process is '**meta-synthesis**'. Meta-synthesis is described as the science of 'summing up' (Light and Pillemer 1984). There are many different approaches to bringing this information together and there is much debate about how this should be done. Some qualitative researchers have argued that it is not appropriate to attempt to bring together the results of research studies at all, and to do so is to strip the work of the depth and insight that it gives and that, as a consequence, all qualitative research should stand alone rather than be combined (Sandelowski *et al.* 1997). Yet, if qualitative research is considered to be generalisable (Morse 1999), then the results have to be viewed in relation to others. Other researchers argue that only papers which have been undertaken using a particular research methodology can be compared

(Jensen and Allen 1996). The principles of meta-analysis, for example, (as referred to in the section below) require that only the results of studies that have used similar methods be combined to be re-analysed statistically. Jensen and Allen (1996) have applied this principle to qualitative research and argue that qualitative research studies using phenomenology could be combined but that the results of a phenomenological study and a grounded theory study could not be. These are complex arguments which you will find debated in the research methodology literature and while they should be acknowledged by the undergraduate researcher, they do not need to be addressed in any detail at this level. If you begin to engage with these arguments, you will enter a very complex area which will take you beyond what can be resolved at undergraduate level.

Three 'advanced' approaches for summing up the literature

There are three well known approaches for summing up the literature: meta-analysis, meta-ethnography and meta-study. These are summarised below. It is important to note that these approaches offer a complex and comprehensive approach to the bringing together of results in a literature review and require the skills of experienced researchers. They are therefore generally beyond the remit of undergraduate study. It is, however, important that the novice researcher recognises the terms that are used and can appreciate the rationale behind these approaches. Following discussion of these approaches, a simplified approach to bringing together literature which has been adapted from the original approaches will be discussed.

Meta-analysis

One approach for combining papers whose results are presented as statistics is meta-analysis. Meta-analysis was developed by Gene Glass in 1976 as a way of integrating and summarising the statistical findings from a body of research. Glass described meta-analysis as 'the analysis of analyses', in which he refers to the 'statistical analysis of a large collection of results from individual studies for the purpose of integrating findings'. This process is referred to as meta-analysis and this approach was undertaken in the analysis described in Chapter 1 in which the results of the individual studies on the drug streptokinase were combined. Meta-analysis was used to combine the results of the studies and was able to demonstrate the effectiveness of the drug, a fact which was not apparent in the individual studies. The statistics from the different papers were combined to reduce the different sets of results to one bigger and more meaningful set of results. A meta-analysis of many different sets of results can only be undertaken if the studies included are similar to each other, so that the combination of results is meaningful. For example, if many RCTs concerning the same topic were identified, it would be possible to combine the results of these studies into one overall result. This has the advantage that the many and possibly varying results from each study are summarised into one study. However, unless the focus or design of all of the studies is the same, combining the results will not be appropriate. It is important to note that meta-analysis refers to the statistical processes that are used to combine the results of the studies and that only studies of a similar nature can be combined. The limitations of using meta-analysis are that it is a complex process which may not be appropriate at undergraduate level. Furthermore, it is an approach that can be used only by those who have exclusively quantitative data of a similar type in their literature review.

Meta-ethnography

A commonly cited approach to the bringing together of qualitative research reports is meta-ethnography. This approach was developed by Noblit and Hare in 1988 and is regularly referred to by those reviewing qualitative data. The authors describe their approach as the 'rigorous procedure for deriving substantive interpretations about any set of ethnographic or interpretive studies' (Noblit and Hare 1988 p. 9). Meta-ethnography can be applied to all qualitative studies that use the same methodology. The results of the qualitative studies are interpreted rather than summarised. The aim is to determine the relationship between the studies so that consistencies and differences are identified. New insights are derived on the topic in question. Meta-ethnography involves determining keywords, phrases, metaphors and ideas that occur in all or some of the studies and to interpret these in the light of those identified in the other studies. Meta-ethnography as defined by Noblit and Hare is a sophisticated approach to the combining of qualitative studies; however, the general principles can be applied to undergraduate study.

Meta-study

A third approach to the bringing together of qualitative research reports is **meta-study** as developed by Paterson *et al.* (2001). The authors offer an approach to the combination of studies that involves close examination of not only the data collected in each study, but also of the method by which the study is undertaken and the underlying theoretical framework upon which the study is based. Clearly this approach demands a high level of expertise and research awareness training on the part of those who undertake it, and as such is generally beyond the remit of undergraduate study. However, as with meta-ethnography, the general principles can be adapted for use by the undergraduate student.

Three established methods have been described which outline the processes of bringing together papers identified for a literature review. It will be evident from the discussion that there are limitations in the application of all of these approaches at undergraduate level. Firstly, none of the approaches can incorporate qualitative, quantitative and discussion papers with each other. Each approach is specific to either quantitative research (meta-analysis) or qualitative research (meta-ethnography or meta-study). Yet, there is growing recognition that literature from many different approaches may inform one research question and to leave out this literature because it is qualitative rather than quantitative (or vice versa) will not enhance the review. In health and social care, students are likely to encounter a wide variety of studies that are relevant to their research question rather than just one type of study. Secondly, all approaches require a high level of research expertise on the part of the researcher, beyond what would be expected at undergraduate level.

A simplified approach

An approach for summing up the literature that is suitable for those new to the literature review process will now be outlined. This method is adapted from the approach given by Paterson *et al.* (2001) and aims to combine the results of studies that have very different research methods in a meaningful way in a literature review.

Providing a summary of your information

The first step is to be able to summarise the content of all the papers and studies that you have. You need to become familiar with all of the information that you have and be able to provide a description of all of the studies and other information you have identified, in chronological order, noting the strengths and limitations of each. You will then be able to give an overall summary of the information you have found. You might find it useful to compile a table to assist you in this process, an example is given in Table 6.1:

Table 6.1 Summarising your information

Author/date	Aim of study/ paper	Type of study/ information	Main findings/ conclusions	Strengths and limitations
Brown/2006	To explore student views of campus life	Questionnaire study	35% of students preferred campus-based universities	Random sample of students not obtained. Very low response rate
George/2005	To express opinion on campus life	Expert opinion	Campus-based universities prevent integration into the community	Anecdotal opinion only

The main purpose of this description is to enable you to get a good understanding of the studies you have and the different approaches used in each one. Thorne *et al.* (2004) describe this process as a 'meta-summary'. It is useful because you cannot begin to compare one study with another until you have a good understanding of the content of each of the studies. As your understanding of the papers develops, you might find that the papers are more specific or actually discuss a different aspect of your research question than you were given at first impression. Be prepared to keep altering your perception of each paper. There are similarities here with the process of qualitative data analysis in which it is critical to achieve a thorough comprehension of the data before they are analysed further (Morse 1994). It is important when undertaking a literature review that you achieve this familiarity with the research and other published material that relates to your research question before you begin to combine the results of these papers.

Comparing and contrasting the results of each study

The second step is to compare and contrast the research studies and other published material that you have described. At this stage you move beyond a straightforward description of the papers towards an integration and interpretation of what the papers mean as a whole, taking into account any similarities and inconsistencies.

Assigning codes

Your first task is to go to the results sections of each research paper, or to the general discussion section if the paper is not a report of research findings, and to assign codes to the main findings/discussion point. If you have predominantly research papers, then you can code the main findings. If you have mainly discussion papers or other reports, you can assign codes to the main discussion points. You may be able to summarise the main outcome of the paper in one word and in which case this will be your first code. The codes should be words that summarise the main point that is made in that particular section and should be written in pencil beside the relevant section so that it is easy to keep a record of the codes you are making. You should go through all of your papers undertaking this method until you have assigned codes to all the results/discussion sections of the papers. For example, let's say you have three papers that explore women's experience of terminating a pregnancy. Each of these papers is qualitative. As you read through the papers you identify the main codes: for example, patient uncertainty as to whether they are doing the right thing, concern for future pregnancies and so on.

Developing themes

Once you have completed all the coding, consider how many times you have assigned the same code to different papers. This will give you an indication of the themes that are emerging from your information. Group together all the codes that are the same or similar so that you can see patterns developing in the coding system. Codes that are identical or similar can be grouped together and referred to as a theme. You can give a name to this theme. The name should reflect the content of the theme. It is advisable to keep the original documents to hand at this point – do not put them to one side as you will need to refer back to them to check for accuracy of the coding. Continue this process of assigning each code into a theme until all your codes have been assigned and you will have a small number of themes with provisional names. It is important to emphasise at this point that the names of the themes, and indeed the codes that make up the themes, are provisional at this stage of the process. For example, one theme might be patient uncertainty as to the nature of their decision.

Comparing the codes and themes

The next step is to revisit each theme and check two things: first, that the name of the theme is fitting to all of the codes that have been assigned to it and, second, that there are no coded sections of results which, on closer analysis, would be better suited to a different theme. Lincoln and Guba (1985 p. 342) describe how this 'dynamic working back and forth' gives the researcher confidence that the development of themes is robust and open to scrutiny. Please note that Lincoln and Guba refer to themes as categories. You will need to check and re-check the accuracy of your coding and theme development.

Close scrutiny of your codes and themes

It is at this point that the similarities and differences in the findings of your review will begin to emerge. Look closely at the themes you are developing and begin to consider how they are linked together. This is why it is important to keep the original documents near to hand as you may need to refer back to them to check the information or to seek further information that becomes required as your analysis progresses. You will find that you have further questions that you want to ask of the papers you have and will need easy access to them. For example, you might find that the experience of women who undergo a termination of pregnancy differs widely. However, on closer scrutiny, you identify that the age and marital status of the women seem to be linked to their experiences.

Working with codes and themes that do not support each other

You might find that you have individual codes or whole themes that do not support each other. The first thing to do is to consider the context of each paper, together with the strengths and limitations of the research approaches undertaken. You need to focus on your critical appraisal of each paper at this point, as you need to assess the strength of the evidence in addressing your particular question. The rationale behind a literature review is that all the relevant literature is reviewed so that you can see each piece of literature in the context of the other available literature, and that differences and similarities in the results can be compared. When you encounter literature that presents a different picture to that given by the previous literature you examined, it is important to document this carefully. Consider why this may be so. What were the differences in the pieces of research undertaken that may account for the different findings? Refer back to the critical appraisal you have undertaken. Is one piece of evidence stronger than the other?

For example, one small-scale study carried out on a small convenience sample of participants might demonstrate different results from that obtained in a larger-scale study undertaken on a more representative sample. You would be more likely to give greater weight to the results of the larger study. The differences in the results might be explained by the sample sizes used. Alternatively, one study set in an inner city area might give very different results to a study undertaken in a rural area. Again, you would consider the relevance of these factors when considering the meaning of the results and you would consider which study setting is most applicable to your review.

Discussion of the strength of evidence

You will probably consider giving more weight to the research that provides stronger evidence than the weaker paper. You may be able to account for the differences by examining the paper in closer detail; however, if no explanation is available, then you need to present the differing accounts and say that you cannot explain them. It is important to describe the differences in results that you find and not to attempt to hide these in order to make your results appear to be more coherent. If all the data suggest different things, document this and say that you cannot reach firm conclusions from the data that you have.

It is important to remember that there will always be inconsistencies that you cannot simply explain away. In such cases, you need to state that the findings of different studies do not appear to lead to the same conclusions and that it is beyond the scope of your review to explain this. Remember to include evidence of critical appraisal when you introduce each new paper that you include in your review.

You can also compare the results of research reports with non-research papers in this way, but again the contexts of both must be fully acknowledged. For example, a discussion paper by a leading expert might argue one point, but this point may not be borne out in the actual research studies which have addressed the same issues. You are likely to find research reports that contradict the opinion of an expert in the research topic area and vice versa. Consider again the widely opposing views of two leading environmentalists, David Bellamy and George Monbiot (*Guardian* 2005). Again, when this is the case you need to consider which is the stronger evidence, expert opinion or a research study? Unless there are many identifiable flaws in the study, or you are specifically looking at expert opinion as part of your review, you are likely to conclude that the study provides the strongest evidence.

Be aware of results that appear too neat

It would be unusual if you were able to develop codes and themes that presented an overall seemless picture in which there was no contradictory data. Expect some results that do not fit in with your overall picture.

Be creative!

The interesting part of this process is that the codes and themes can be named as you deem appropriate. This is your analysis – be creative, but do be sure that you can justify the names of the themes and the relevant inclusion of coded data. At the end of this process you should have a firmed-up set of themes with names that convey the meaning of the codes within them.

For example, a theme might be named 'anxiety about hospital admission'. The codes within this theme that you identified from your literature might be 'patients' fear of hospital', 'distress at unfamiliar procedures' and so on.

You should begin to feel comfortable with the emerging picture you have developed and confident to explain how you developed the codes and themes. You might find it helpful to continue using a chart to demonstrate the codes and themes you develop. This will enable you to keep a track of *how* you developed the codes and themes from the original results. You are advised to keep a record of the charts you have developed for the general description of the studies and a record of the ways in which you coded and themed your data and include these records in an appendix of your final dissertation.

This approach is similar to that carried out by qualitative researchers when they analyse qualitative data, for example the methods outlined by Lincoln and Guba (1985). Paterson *et al.* (2001 p. 55) describe this process of coding and comparing studies in a literature review as the 'comparative analysis' of research findings. Through this process, the relationship of one study to another becomes apparent and there is continuous comparative analysis of the texts until a comprehensive understanding of the phenomena is reached (Paterson *et al.* 2001 p. 64).

One of the main differences between the approach to meta-synthesis advocated in this book and the approaches developed by Paterson *et al.* (2001) and Noblit and Hare (1988) is the amount of detail that can be given to the analysis and synthesis of the results in each of the papers. For example, Paterson *et al.* (2001) recommend that two or three people code each paper, in order to generate maximum insight about the meaning of the paper. At undergraduate level this is not likely to be possible as resources do not permit; however, you might find it useful to discuss this process with your project supervisor or ask a friend to look over your ideas. If you do this, remember to write this up in your methods section.

Writing up your results

It is important to present your findings of your literature review as just that – your findings. You should make this clear when you write up your review. They should be written up clearly in a section entitled results/findings, just as you would find the results section in a piece of primary research.

The results of your literature review are the final themes that you develop from the coding you have undertaken. Once you have coded all your results, and have developed your themes, you will be able to explore the content of your themes in greater detail. You then need to consider how these themes address your research question. You should have been considering this point throughout the entire research process and may even have amended your research question if it seemed likely that most of your literature was leading you towards one particular area, and away from your initial research question.

Telling a story with your data

Once you have established your main themes, you need to present these in the most appropriate way to address your review question. You are likely to divide up your results section into a series of headings which relate to the main themes you have identified. You may begin the results section by describing the main finding or theme – that is the theme which seems the most relevant to addressing your question or which contains codes that occurred most often in your literature. You should include all the research and other information that relates to this theme in this section. You will probably use research papers first followed by non-research papers. You are then likely to find that another theme illustrates an aspect of the first theme you present. Again, you should include all the information relevant to this theme in this section. In this way, you will find that one theme follows on from another and gradually your research question is addressed in different ways by each of the themes you have identified. Your task is to organise these themes into a logical order so that the findings of one theme are then explained in more detail by the next theme and so on. You also need to draw attention to themes that do not fit with the overall picture you are developing. Think of this process as comparable to telling a story – you are explaining how the literature you have identified addresses and sheds light on the research question you have selected.

Incorporating your critical appraisal

As you write up each theme, you need to consider how you will document the process of critical appraisal undertaken for each paper you reviewed. As a general rule, the first time you introduce a paper, you need to give the context for this paper. You need to state the aims of the paper, the methods used and the main findings. You can then give some of the limitations of the paper and comment on the impact that you feel the paper should have in your developing argument. The next time you refer back to this paper, you only need to reference it as the critical appraisal will be cited earlier in the text.

If you do not do this, you will not be able to give information about the source you are using. Compare the following examples:

Example 1: 'Smith 2006 argues that nurses use their professional judgement when assessing wounds . . .' This sentence does not give any reference to the context of the information from which this statement is drawn. There is no indication as to whether Smith is citing his or her opinion, someone else's opinion, or results from a study. You could argue that the statement is misleading.

Compare the above statement with the following:

Example 2: 'Regarding the use of tools for the assessment of wounds, Smith (2006) explored how nurses assess the type of wound dressing they need for a particular patient. He interviewed ten experienced nurses working in a day care centre for older people in an urban hospital in England about their assessment strategies and how they applied these to different patients. He identified that while some nurses relied on the assessment tools available in the clinical area, many nurses relied on their clinical judgement. This was a small study, undertaken by a nurse experienced in the care of older people. All the interviews were tape-recorded and transcribed. However, all participants involved in the study were specialist practitioners with many years of experience. Those with less experience were not invited to participate in the study. The results are therefore not necessarily transferable to other settings.'

Example 2 contains more useful information than Example 1, yet both could be written with reference to the same study. This illustrates the need to give a short critical appraisal of the literature you are using. When you then refer to this paper again, you need only to refer to the author and date of the paper.

The question of what you should do if the evidence you have is of poor quality is important to consider. The Cochrane Collaboration, for example, have strict criteria for the inclusion and exclusion of papers in their reviews, ensuring that only what is considered to be good evidence is included in the final review. However, the implication of this is that much information is excluded from the review. As a new researcher, you are advised to include all the information that you have which is related to your topic but to be clear about the strengths and limitations of this information. This way, all relevant information is included but will not be given equal weight in your review.

What do I do if my information only partially addresses my research question?

Three scenarios are presented below which refer to the extent to which the literature addresses your research question. They are referred to as best-case, middle-case and worst-case scenario. They do not refer to the overall quality of your literature review but to the extent to which the available literature is able to answer the research question you identified.

The best-case scenario

This is that you will have developed a set of categories, or themes that relate to each other and fully address your research question. You are confident that each theme comprises information that is based on strong evidence that is appropriate to answer your research question. You can then write these up, so that they tell a story and explain different aspects of the research question. Even with this best-case scenario, it is unlikely that all of the aspects in each theme fit together – there will always be discrepancies and you will not always be able to explain these. However, you should document these inconsistencies.

The middle-case scenario

This is that you have developed a set of categories or themes that relate in part to the research question or are comprised of evidence that is not very strong. You will need to comment on the strength of the evidence which makes up your theme and the relevance of this literature in addressing the research question. For example, one theme might address your question, but if the theme is composed of weak evidence you need to address this and state that while there is some evidence that addresses your research question, the evidence is not strong and the results do not fully answer your question. You would be able to say that there is weak evidence to support a particular argument, but this cannot be further verified by the data that currently exists. In addition, you might be able to make theoretical arguments about the answer to your research question from the evidence provided. For example, if there is little available evidence on your research topic but there is evidence about a related topic, you might be able to theorise about the application of this knowledge to your topic. Remember that this evidence is not strong, but you might be able to make a good case.

The worst-case scenario

This is that you find that none of your themes address your research question or that the evidence contained within the themes is very weak. For example, if your research question required empirical evidence such as results of primary data to address the question and you were not able to identify any studies involving primary data collection, you would have to conclude that the research question is not answerable. If this is the case, then you need to state that you have comprehensively and systematically undertaken all the steps required to review the literature in an attempt to address the (stated) research question but that the question was not answerable using the literature. This is an important finding in itself and points to the need for a study involving primary data collection in order to find an answer to the question you identified. At under-graduate level you are less likely to be penalised for this; however, for those undertaking postgraduate study, you would be expected to have done a preliminary search of the literature to establish the viability of the research question before you commenced your study.

In reality, you will find that your evidence lies on a continuum where at one end your research question remains fully unresolved, while at the other your research question is completely addressed:

◀ - ▶

Literature reviewed   Literature reviewed
but does not address   completely answers
the research question   the research question

Tips for writing up your synthesis of the literature

1 You need to demonstrate how you developed the themes you describe.
2 Try to link the studies together so that you compare and contrast the studies.
3 Identify which studies/information do not fit into the overall argument you are making.
4 Identify any gaps in the literature which might leave aspects of your research question unanswered.

In summary

Throughout the process of summing up the literature you are seeking to identify common themes that arise from the literature you have identified. You are likely to write up your themes under a series of main headings within which you discuss the main results within that theme. You are seeking to identify how the themes fit together, taking into account the strengths and limitations of the literature from which the themes are comprised. Your task is then to organise your themes so that they relate to each other and follow a logical order. These themes should then be presented in a way that addresses the research question.

Key points

• Your main findings are the results of your literature review.
• Each paper included in your review should be coded in order to identify main themes.

- These themes are then brought together so that one theme expands on and adds insight to another.
- Remember to document where there are gaps in the literature that leave aspects of your question unaddressed.
- Remember to document information that does not fit with the argument you are making.

7

How do I discuss my findings and make recommendations?

*Statement of findings • Strengths and limitations of your study •
Strengths and limitations in relation to other studies • The meaning
of the study within the wider context • Interpreting your results •
Discussion of unanswered questions and future research • Tips for
writing up your discussion section • Key points*

The final stage of your literature review is to relate the main themes you
have identified in your review to a wider context of the area you have
studied. This ultimately means that you have to interpret the meaning of
your results and the implications they have on your area of practice.

It is often reported that writing the discussion section of a dissertation
or literature review is one of the hardest sections to write. Until this
point, you have followed a systematic and logical process which has
resulted in the presentation of the results of your study. How these
results should be incorporated into the wider context can be a daunting
task at the end of a study. If you are submitting your work for an academic degree, you might also be running near to the deadline by which
your work is to be submitted. The most important thing to ensure is that

the claims made in the discussion are actually borne out in the results. You must resist the temptation to make more of the results than the quality of the results allows. If your results are equivocal, you must report this and be prepared to discuss the implications of an inconclusive result. Horton (1995) observed that many discussion sections of research papers made claims and wider generalisations that were not warranted by the results of the study. In doing so, the validity of the whole study is put into question.

Doherty and Smith (1999) suggest the following approach for the structure of a discussion:

- statement of principal findings
- strengths and limitations of the study
- strengths and limitations in relation to other studies, discussing in particular any differences in results
- the meaning of the study
- discussion of unanswered questions and future research.

Each of these aspects will be discussed in turn below.

Statement of findings

It is important to remember that you should not repeat your results section in your discussion, but you should attempt to summarise your findings in one or two sentences that convey the general meaning of what your review has found. You are likely to require several attempts at the wording of this before you communicate succinctly the meaning of your findings. Try different ways, look objectively at the meaning of what you have written and consider whether you have captured the essence of your results in these sentences. It is appropriate to make generalisations about your findings when you are summarising your results, for example, 'most social workers were happy to undertake additional duties however' . . . but you need to ensure that your generalisations convey the meaning of your findings. The important thing is that you capture the meaning of your results in a few sentences.

Strengths and limitations of your study

It is important to acknowledge the strengths and limitations of your literature review. This is because it acknowledges to the reader the draw-backs to your research and enables the results to be placed in context. In the same way as you have undertaken a critical appraisal of the information upon which your literature review is based, it is also necessary to undertake a critical appraisal of your own work. Some possible limitations to your literature review might be as follows: that as a novice researcher your approach to the identification, critique and bringing together of the literature may not have been as thorough as that of a more experienced researcher. In addition, there will have been time and resource limitations to your study. You are unlikely to have had the financial resources to commit to the study which might have enabled you to retrieve more literature via inter-library loans, or visiting libraries further afield. Additional finances might have enabled you to employ the assistance of other researchers who would have aided you in the search, critique and bringing together of the literature. Your study is also likely to have been limited due to time restraints. At this stage you could also mention what you have learnt from undertaking this research process and how you would approach a similar study in the future.

Strengths and limitations in relation to other studies

Given that your study is a review of the literature and you are not collect-ing new data, you are probably less likely to discuss the strengths and limitations of your study in relation to other studies unless you have encountered another systematic review. In this case, you can relate the strengths and weakness of your methodology to the other reviews.

The meaning of the study within the wider context

The next step is to set your results within the wider context of your area of health and social care practice. For the researcher undertaking a literature review as a component of an academic degree, it is usually a requirement of the degree that the review relates specifically to the area of practice in which a qualification is sought. It is therefore important to explain the meaning of the results to the practice setting.

This requires you to start focussing outwards and begin to consider how the main themes you have identified relate to the wider context in which your research question is located. For example, your results might suggest that patients/clients prefer to administer their own medication whilst in hospital; however, this might be in conflict with local policy. Or your results might suggest that a particular professional role is valued and considered to provide a useful contribution to patient/client care but that this is not appreciated by the professional bodies who are considering removing this professional role. If you have related your literature review to a particular theoretical framework, now is the time to refer back to this and review your research in the light of this framework.

Think widely about what is happening in the area in which you are engaged in terms of policy, Government White Papers, consultation papers, professional guidelines, National Service Frameworks, and so on. You may have mentioned these in your introduction but you can refer back to them in your discussion in the light of the findings you have made. Talk to experts in the area to check you haven't missed any major developments that link into your topic area. Scan the 'news' sections of your professional journal for debate that might add additional context to your review.

Interpreting your results

You also need to consider carefully how you interpret your results. There is some concern that researchers interpret their findings too widely and make assertions that are not justified from the results obtained in the study. If your results are inconclusive it is important to restate this rather than try to make the results appear to show something that they do not. Be prepared to discuss what you have found. Refer to the findings specifically rather than making generalised statements such as 'all social workers do xx', if your data do not bear this out. Do not be tempted to exaggerate your findings so that your argument flows better. There is some current concern that researchers who place too much of their own interpretation on the results risk losing their discussion to subjective speculation thus jeopardising the importance of their results

(Doherty and Smith 1999). This will be identified by those who examine your work and your findings may be discredited. On the other hand, you do need to provide some interpretation of your findings and put your own judgement on them. There is little point to a discussion section if you merely repeat the main findings of the study and do not exercise any judgement or interpretation of the findings (Skelton and Edwards 2000).

For the purpose of your literature review, you need to demonstrate that you can make sense of what you have found and make appropriate reference to the possible meaning of your findings to the wider context. You should be able to identify some clear recommendations for practice. Remember that these arise from your own original work and so you can be bold about the assertions you make; however, you need to ensure that your recommendations arise directly from your discussion. Recommendations can be listed clearly as bullet points, for example.

Discussion of unanswered questions and future research

As has been discussed previously, it is very likely that when you undertake your literature review, you will not be able to answer your research question in full. You are likely only to be able to partially address the research question you have identified. This is because of the limitations in the data, or literature, you have collected. This may be due to *your* limitations as a researcher and the time restrictions you had, or it may be that there is little published information about your topic. It is therefore appropriate that you summarise what your research has failed to address and discuss the possibilities for future research. Depending on the strengths of the literature you have identified, possibilities for further research might be either a further review of the literature or primary research for which your research has identified the need.

Tips for writing up your discussion section

1 Restate your research question when you commence this section.
2 Avoid repetition of the results section.

3 Do not add new ideas generated from your data to this section.
4 Be confident about the points you make. Remember this is your study and you are qualified to make assertions about practice and further research if they are justified.
5 You do not need to critique the research you refer to in the discussion but demonstrate the link between your findings and related literature.
6 Finally, be clear as to how your findings have addressed the research question.

Key points

1 Ensure your discussion is an accurate reflection of the results.
2 Summarise your main findings in the discussion section, but briefly!
3 Summarise the quality of the studies you included.
4 Refer to related literature to set your study in context.
5 Discuss any unanswered questions and recommendations for future research.

8

How do I present my literature review?

*A suggested structure • Top tips for writing up your literature review
• Key points in presenting your literature review*

Once you have undertaken all the work required to complete your literature review, you have one important task left. That is to present your work in a way that reflects the hard graft you done. The way in which your work is presented is very important. If you submit a carefully prepared report of your literature review, you will give the reader the impression that you have undertaken this piece of work in a careful manner. A hastily prepared report will give the opposite impression. It is also important that you follow a logical structure in the presentation of your work, so that the marker can see at a glance that you have been methodical in your approach to your study. Remember that if you do not write up any aspect of your literature review, the reader will assume that this aspect was not addressed in your work.

A suggested structure

The following structure is suggested as a plan for your literature review.

Title page

If you are submitting your literature review as part of an academic degree, you are advised to consult the guidance notes concerning the information required on your title page.

Acknowledgements

It is customary to acknowledge your supervisor and any other professionals who have assisted your research in addition to others from whom you have received support.

Contents page

This should include appropriate reference to page numbers. Include reference to appendices.

Lists of tables and figures

Include these, where appropriate, to illustrate your work.

Abstract

This is a very brief summary of the whole dissertation including the results and conclusions. Make sure it is an accurate summary of your research and your findings.

Introduction

This usually includes your rationale for undertaking the study, provides an overview of the subject area, and outlines your key research question/s. Remember that you do not have to include critical appraisal in this section. It is acceptable to summarise the main research in the area using key references.

Methods

This section incorporates every aspect of the systematic approach you have undertaken in order to achieve a comprehensive review of the literature. It is important that you document clearly how you undertook the steps you took. The reader needs to know that you undertook a comprehensive and systematic approach to your literature review, and the only way to determine this is to give a full account of your literature review process. Do not leave this to chance. If you do not document a process that was undertaken, the reader will be given the impression that this process was not undertaken. The methods section will usually commence with how you identified your research question. Discuss the rationale for your research question and explore its origins. It is often useful to describe a critical incident that occurred in your practice which sparked your interest in the topic, if this is relevant. Remember to justify your use of a literature review as your chosen research methodology. What was it about your research question that made it suitable for literature review rather than primary data collection? You should then document how you searched for appropriate literature. You are advised to include a report of the search terms you used and your search strategy. You should then document how this literature was critiqued and justify your choice of critical appraisal tools. Finally, you need to document how you brought this information together. Present information in a graph or chart if this is appropriate. Overall, your methods section will contribute a large portion of the complete review and is likely to amount to approximately one-fifth to one-quarter of the total word count.

Results

This section incorporates the main themes/results that you have identified from the literature review. You are likely to commence with the most dominant theme and discuss the following themes thereafter. Remember to discuss all your themes in a logical order, bringing out the similarities and inconsistencies in the data that you have.

Discussion

This section provides an interpretation of your results in the light of other related literature. It is important to ensure that your discussion draws on all aspects of your results section and that you do not add new information to your discussion section. In addition, you should set your results in context by exploring the limitations of your review. You should also discuss how your role as a novice researcher affected the ways in which the project was undertaken. Finally, you should discuss your role as researcher, how you have learnt from this role and what you would do differently next time.

References

This must be 100 per cent correct. You should reference every piece of published material to which you referred in your review. If you have used secondary references make sure you reference these as such. If your literature review is being submitted as part of an academic award, it is important to refer to the referencing guidelines issues by the academic institution to which you will be submitting it.

Bibliography

You should also cite the books and texts to which you referred but did not make direct reference to, if you are required to do so by your academic institution.

Appendices

These should contain any information that is relevant to your literature review but which is not contained in the main body of the text. For example, the processes by which you devised your themes when analysing the results of your literature search could be written up in the appendix. In addition, letters from practitioners or other professionals who assisted you in your research can be placed in the appendix. It is important to number each appendix.

Top tips for writing up your literature review

1 Set your research question as the header or footer on your screen and adhere to it at all times.
2 Do not get sidetracked by unrelated issues and unrelated literature.
3 Keep a record of all references you use from the beginning of the literature review process.
4 Keep an up-to-date back-up of your work.
5 Above all, make sure you answer the research question!

Key points in presenting your literature review

1 Your review should be coherent, systematic and clear.
2 Ensure that you follow your research question throughout your review.
3 Every section that you write should relate to your original question. If it does not, leave it out.
4 Avoid the term 'the author' if it is not clear to whom you are referring.
5 Reference your sources appropriately.

Commonly asked questions

How should I structure my work? • Should I use first or third person? • How should I use references? • How do I avoid plagiarism and misrepresentation? • What is the role of my supervisor?

Students frequently ask the following questions of the academic supervisors overseeing their literature review. The answers below are not intended to be exhaustive but should act as a guide to your study.

How should I structure my work?

The structure for a literature review should be coherent, systematic and clear (Hart 2003). This cannot be emphasised enough. It is very common, even for those who have undertaken a systematic approach to the process of undertaking their dissertation, to find that this is not demonstrated through the writing up of their dissertation. One common occurrence is that the novice reviewer sets themselves a research question but then does not address the question. There can be a few reasons why this happens. Firstly, the reviewer might not realise the importance of the research question. Secondly, the reviewer might encounter interesting information about a similar but not related topic and get sidetracked by this information. If this happens, you are advised, if circumstances permit, to alter your research question so that you can focus your research on a topic that has become more relevant to you. The worst thing you can do is to keep the research question unchanged but persevere with the literature that has caught your attention, if this does not relate to the question.

It is very important to keep your research question in mind throughout the whole process of undertaking your literature review. Some people find it useful to write the literature review question as a header on the entire document so that at every stage of the writing, they can refer to their question. You also need to ensure that each chapter links into the previous chapter and then on to the next chapter. This can be achieved by providing a summary at the end of each chapter (a few sentences only) and then making specific reference as to how the next chapter takes the reader forward. For example, at the end of the first chapter, you might write something like: 'In this chapter I have argued why it is important to involve the social worker in the development of local policy for social housing. My research question seeks to address how this involvement can be achieved. In order to do this I intend to undertake a review of the literature. The methods I used to achieve this are outlined in the next chapter.'

Should I use first or third person?

Students are often concerned about whether they should write in the first or third person. That is, whether they should write 'I searched through CINAHL' or 'the author searched through CINAHL'. You might be tempted to use the third person form, thinking that it is somehow more objective and more appropriate for an academic piece of work. However, this is not always the case. The use of the first person for academic writing, in certain instances, has long been advocated (Webb 1992, Hamil 1999, Hart 2003). This is because if you call yourself 'the author' it can become confusing and it is sometimes difficult for the reader to know whether you are talking about yourself or another author. Therefore, rather than adding to academic clarity, the use of the third person can cause the writing style to become confused and difficult to follow. Webb (1992) even goes so far as to describe writing in the third person to be, in some instances, a form of deception, as the thinking of the author is masked and not made explicit. In principle, you are advised to use the first person form throughout your literature review. This is because when you are writing up your literature review, it is important that the process you undertook is explicit. You need to write in a way that reflects the experience you have had in undertaking the research process. The easiest way to achieve this is to write in the first person, so that it is clear who undertook the search, who undertook the critical appraisal, and so on. For example, 'I undertook an electronic literature search' is clearer than 'an electronic literature search was undertaken'. This is especially important when you are reviewing the literature because you are likely to be referring to many different authors and clarity is crucial. The passive voice can be useful in cases where you need to maintain anonymity, for example, 'I was informed that . . .' is preferable to 'XX informed me that. . .'. In summary, you need to ensure that your work is clear. If there is any uncertainty about who you are referring to when you state 'the author', you should use 'I' statements and restrict use of the term 'the author' for those whose work you are referring to.

How should I use references?

References should be used to provide evidence for the points you make throughout your literature review. Your main use of references is likely to be in your results section when you present the literature you have identified. In this section, you will need to cite the reference to the literature to which you are referring and then to describe how you have critically appraised this reference.

In the other sections of your literature review (in your introduction, methodology and discussion sections, for example), it will normally be sufficient to cite an appropriate reference to illustrate the points you make. However, it is important to make sure that you reference appropriately. Make sure you select a reference that illustrates the point you are making and that it is clear which aspect of your argument you are reinforcing with this reference. For example, if you are referring to the origins of evidence-based practice, you would be likely to refer to the work of Sackett *et al.* (1996). This is because their work was fundamental in establishing this approach to health and social care. If you cite a lesser known author who has discussed evidence-based practice and do not refer to the originators of the approach, you will not appear to have a comprehensive or thorough understanding of your topic. Therefore, it is important that you avoid the temptation to cite any reference that seems to reinforce the points you are making but that you trace the most relevant sources that reinforce your argument. In this way, you need to undertake a mini critical appraisal of the references you use so that you can be sure you are using the most appropriate references. It is common for those new to academic writing to perceive that any reference will enhance their written work as long as it relates in some way to the points they are making. In reality, if you cite an inappropriate reference, this will detract from the quality of your work. In principle, make sure the reference you cite is authoritative for the points you are making.

How do I avoid plagiarism and misrepresentation?

Plagiarism refers to the presentation of the ideas and published material of someone else as if they were your own. This can be confusing for the novice researcher especially as the entire process of undertaking a literature review involves representing the work of others, analysing and summarisng this work in order to determine the contribution of this work in answering your research question. How you represent the work of others is clearly very important. There are a few general principles to follow:

1 When you refer to someone's work, always acknowledge the author, even if you are not making a direct quotation. The careful process of critical appraisal should lead you to be able to summarise the work of another researcher or practitioner in a way that does not lead to misrepresentation. It is important that you stay true to the literature that you have, so that you represent the information that you have appropriately. Be sure to document all your references carefully as you go through the process of the literature review, so that all the sources you use are clearly referenced and your own ideas are identifiable from those of others.

2 Direct quotations of someone else's work must always be in quotation marks.

3 If you are referring to general ideas, you do not always need to provide a reference. However, if you do provide a reference, try to ensure that the reference is appropriate. For example, 'it is now well established that smoking causes cancer'. An appropriate reference should be made

to the original studies that identified this link rather than any later commentary on the link between smoking and cancer. If you do refer to later commentaries on the link between smoking and cancer, you would need to discuss in which context you are using the reference.

What is the role of my supervisor?

If you are undertaking a literature review as part of an academic degree, you are likely to be allocated a supervisor. Your supervisor for your literature review is there as a resource, guide and support for your studies. He or she will not take the lead on the study and will expect you to determine the steps you need to take to complete your review. Your supervisor might have a professional interest in your area of study, but this will not necessarily be the case. It is more important that your supervisor is familiar with the process of undertaking literature reviews than familiar with your topic area itself. This is because your supervisor will oversee that you are following the most appropriate ways to address your research question, rather than assisting you with the actual answer to that question.

When you begin the supervisory relationship, you are advised to discuss with your supervisor how you would like the supervision process to proceed. Discuss how you work, whether you respond well to deadlines or are sufficiently well motivated to set your own deadlines. Discuss when your supervisor would like to see drafts of your work and obtain information regarding the availability of your supervisor. Be clear regarding your expectations of your supervisor's role and where you should obtain extra support, for example on information specifically related to your topic. Finally, consult carefully any guidance notes you may have on the role of the supervisor within your own institution.

Glossary

Abstract: A summary of a research or discussion paper.

Action research: A study carried out in a setting in which the results are implemented and evaluated within that setting.

Case control study: A study in which people with a specific condition (cases) are compared to people without this condition (controls) to compare the frequency of the occurrence of the exposure that might have caused the disease.

CONSORT statement: A statement that describes the information that should be included in the report of a trial.

Critical appraisal: A process by which the quality of evidence is assessed.

Critical appraisal tool: A checklist used to assess the quality of evidence.

Cohort study: A study in which two or more groups or cohorts are followed up to examine whether exposures measured at the beginning lead to outcomes, such as disease.

Confidence interval: Usually (but arbitrarily) 95 per cent confidence intervals. A reasonable, though strictly incorrect interpretation, is that the 95 per cent confidence interval gives the range in which the population effect lies.

Descriptive statistics: Statistics such as means, medians, standard deviations, which describe aspects of the data, such as central tendency (mean or median) or its dispersion (standard deviation).

Discussion paper: A paper presenting an argument or discussion.

Dissertation: A document presenting the main findings from a piece of academic work.

Empirical research: Research which is based on observation or experiment. The opposite of this is theoretical research.

Essay: A short piece of academic writing on a selected topic.

Ethnography: Qualitative research approach which involves the study of culture/way of life of participants.

Evidence-based practice: Practice which is based on the best available evidence, moderated by patient preferences.

Generalise: To apply the findings of a study to another population.

Grounded theory: Qualitative research approach that involves the generation of theory.

Hierarchy of evidence: A grading system for assessing the quality of evidence.

Inclusion and exclusion criteria: Criteria that are set in order to focus the searching strategy for a literature review.

Inferential statistics: Statistics that are used to infer findings from the sample population to the wider population, usually meaning statistical tests.

Meta-analysis: A process by which quantitative data with similar properties is combined to produce a weighted average of all the results.

Meta-ethnography: A process by which qualitative data is combined.

Meta-study: A process by which qualitative data is combined.

Narrative review: A literature review that is not undertaken according to a predefined and systematic approach.

Non-empirical evidence: Evidence that is not based on the findings of research.

Null hypothesis: States that there is no difference between a treatment group and a control group in a study. Researchers often seek to reject the null hypothesis.

Phenomenology: Qualitative research approach in which the participants 'lived experience' is explored.

Primary study: A study that collects original data (primary data) from participants, often patients or clients.

Purposive sampling: Sampling strategy used by qualitative researchers who are looking for a sample that is 'fit for the purposes' of the study in question.

p values: p for probability. The p value is the probability of observing results or results more extreme than those observed if the null hypothesis was true.

Qualitative research: Research that involves an in-depth understanding of the reasons for and meanings of human behaviour.

Quantitative research: Research that involves counting.

Random sampling: A sampling strategy in which everyone in a given population has an equal chance of being selected and that probability is independent of any other person selected.

Randomisation: The process of allocating individuals randomly to groups in a trial.

Randomised controlled trial. A trial which has randomly assigned groups in order to determine the effectiveness of an intervention(s) which is given to one/two of the groups.

Research question: A question set by researchers at the outset of a study, to be addressed in the study.

Research methodology: The process undertaken in order to address the research question.

Secondary sources: A source which is not derived from an eyewitness account of a situation.

Snowball sampling: A sampling strategy in which who/what is involved in the study (sample) is determined according to the needs of the study as the investigation progresses.

Stratification: The sample is divided into groups that have the same value, for example, stratifying by age means putting people of the same age or age group together.

Systematic review: A review of the literature that is undertaken according to a defined and systematic approach.

References

Asaria P and MacMahon E (2006) Measles in the United Kingdom. Can we eradicate it by 2010? *British Medical Journal* 333: 890–5

Barbour RS (2001) Checklists for improving rigour in qualitative research. A case of the tail wagging the dog? *British Medical Journal* 322: 1115–17

Barroso J, Gollop CJ, Sandelowski M, Meynell J, Pearce PF, Collins LJ (2003) The challenges of searching for and retrieving qualitative studies, *Western Journal of Nursing Research* 25(2): 153–78

Boynton PM and Greenhalgh T (2004) Hands-on guide to questionnaire research; Selecting, designing, and developing your questionnaire, *British Medical Journal* 328: 1312–15

Bradshaw A (2001) *The Nurse Apprentice 1860–1977*. Ashgate Publishing

Cottrell S (2005) *Critical Thinking Skills*. Palgrave Macmillan: Basingstoke

Crombie I (2006) *Pocket Guide to Critical Appraisal*. BMJ Publishing Group: London

Demicheli V, Jefferson T, Rivetti A, Price D (2006) Vaccines for measles, mumps and rubella in children, *The Cochrane Database of Systematic Reviews* Issue 2, The Cochrane Collaboration. John Wiley and Sons

Doherty M and Smith R (1999) The case for structuring the discussion of scientific papers, *British Medical Journal* 318: 1224–5

Doll R and Hill AB (1954) The mortality of doctors in relation to their smoking habits, *British Medical Journal* 228: 1451–5

Easterbrook PJ, Berlin JA, Gopalan R, Matthews DR (1991) Publication bias in clinical trials, *Lancet* 337(8746): 867–72

Evans D (2002) Database searches for qualitative research, *Journal of the Medical Library Association* 90: 290–293

Evans D (2003) Hierarchy of evidence: a framework for ranking evidence evaluating health care interventions, *Journal of Clinical Nursing* 12: 77–84

Faggiano F, Vigna-Taglianti FD, Versino E, Zambon A, Borraccino A, Lemma P (2006) School based prevention for illicit drug use, *The Cochrane Database of Systematic Reviews* Issue 3, The Cochrane Collaboration. John Wiley and Sons

Finfgeld DL (2003) Metasynthesis: the state of the art so far, *Qualitative Health Research* 13(7): 893–904

Fink A (2005) *Conducting Research Literature Reviews*. SAGE Publications: Thousand Oaks

Giustini D (2005) How Google is changing medicine, *British Medical Journal* 331: 1487–8

Glaser BG and Strauss A (1967) The constant comparative method of qualitative analysis, *The discovery of grounded theory*, Aldine: Chicago

Glass GV (Ed.) (1976) *Evaluation Studies Review Annual*, vol. 1 SAGE Publications: Beverly Hills, CA

Greenhalgh T (1997) How to read a paper. Papers that summarise other papers, *British Medical Journal* 315: 672–5

Greenhalgh T and Peacock R (2005) Effectiveness and efficiency of search methods in systematic reviews of complex evidence: audit of primary sources, *British Medical Journal* 331: 1064–5

Greenhalgh T and Taylor R (1997) How to read a paper. Papers that go beyond numbers (qualitative research), *British Medical Journal* 315: 740–3

Guardian (2005) Comment, Tuesday May 10

Guba EG and Lincoln YS (1995) *Fourth Generation Evaluation*. SAGE: Newbury Park, CA

Hamil C (1999) Academic writing in the first person: a guide for undergraduates, *Nursing Standard* July 21–27, vol. 13: 44

Hart C (2003) *Doing a Literature Review*. SAGE: London

Hawker S, Payne S, Kerr C, Hardey M, Powell J (2002) Appraising the evidence. Reviewing disparate data systematically, *Qualitative Health Research* 12(9): 1284–99

Hek G, Langton H, Blunden G (2000) Systematically searching and reviewing literature, *Nurse Researcher* 7(3) Spring

Horsburgh D (2003) Evaluation of qualitative research, *Journal of Clinical Nursing* 12: 307–12

Horton R (1995) The rhetoric of research, *British Medical Journal* 310: 985–7

Jensen LA and Allen MN (1996) Meta-synthesis of qualitative findings, *Qualitative Health Research* 6(4): 553–60

Katrak P, Bialocerkowski AE, Massy-Westropp N, Kumar S, Grimmer KA (2004) A systematic review of the content of critical appraisal tools, *BMC Medical Research Methodology* 4(22)

Knipschild P (1994) Systematic reviews: some examples, *British Medical Journal* 309: 719–21

Kvale S (1989) *Issues of validity in qualitative research*. SAGE Publications: Thousand Oaks, California

Law R (2004) From research topic to research question: a challenging process, *Nurse Researcher* 11(4): 54–66

Light RJ and Pillemer DB (1984) *Summing up: the Science of Reviewing Research*. Harvard University Press: Cambridge, MA

Lincoln YS and Guba EG (1985) *Naturalistic Inquiry*. SAGE: Beverly Hills, CA

Littleton D, Marsalis S, Zimmaro Bliss D (2004) Searching the literature by design, *Western Jourrnal of Nursing Research* 26(8): 892–908

Lloyd Jones M (2004) Application of systematic review methods to qualitative research. Practical issues, *Journal of Advanced Nursing* 48(3): 271–8

MacAuley D, McCrum E, Brown C (1998) Randomised controlled trial of the READER method of critical appraisal in general practice, *British Medical Journal* 316: 1134–7

Moher D, Schulz KF, Altman DG (2001) The CONSORT statement. Revised recommendations for improving the quality of reports of parallel groups randomised trials, *Annals of Internal Medicine* 134: 657–62

Montori VM, Wilczynski NL, Morgan D, Haynes RB (2004) Optimal search strategies for retrieving systematic reviews from Medline: an analytic survey, *British Medical Journal* 330: 7482.

Morse JM (1994) 'Emerging from the data'. The cognitive processes of analysis in qualitative inquiry. In *Critical issues in qualitative research methods.* SAGE: London

Morse JM (1999) Qualitative generalisability, *Qualitative Health Research* 9(1): 5–6

Morse JM, Barrett M, Mayan M, Olson K, Spiers J (2002) Verification strategies for establishing reliability and validity, *Qualitative Research International Journal of Qualitative Studies* 1, issue 2

Mulrow CD (1994) Systemic reviews: rationale for systematic reviews, *British Medical Journal* 309: 597–9

Mulrow CD, Cook DJ, Davidoff F (1997) Systematic reviews. Critical links in the great chain of evidence, *Annals of Internal Medicine* 126(5): 389–91

Noblit GW and Hare RD (1988) Meta-ethnography, synthesising qualitative studies, *Qualitative Research Methods*, Volume 11. SAGE: London

Oppenheim AN (1992) *Questionnaire design, interviewing and attitude measurement.* London: Continuum

Oxman AD (1994) Systematic reviews, checklists for review articles, *British Medical Journal* 309: 648–51

Paterson B, Thorne S, Canam C, Jillings C (2001) *Metastudy of Qualitative Health Research.* SAGE Publications: Thousand Oaks, California

Pauling L (1986) *How to Live Longer and Feel Better.* Oregon State University Press: Corvallis, Oregon

Petrovic M, Roberts R, Ramsay M (2001) Second dose of measles, mumps, and rubella vaccine: questionnaire survey of health professionals, *British Medical Journal*, 322: 82–5

Polit DF and Beck C (2005) *Essentials of Nursing Research.* Lippincott Williams and Wilkins: Baltimore

Popay J, Rogers A, Williams G (1998) Rationale and standards for the systematic review of qualitative literature in health services research, *Qualitative Health Research* 8(3): 341–51

Prochaska JO, Norcross JC, and DiClemente, CC (1994) *Changing for Good.* William Morrow: New York

Rochon PA, Gurwitz JH, Sykora K, Mamdani M, Streiner DL, Garfinkel S, Normand ST, Anderson GM (2005) Reader's guide to critical appraisal of cohort studies. 1. Role and design, *British Medical Journal* 330: 895–7

Russell CK and Gregory DM (2003) Evaluation of qualitative research studies, *Evidence Based Nursing* 6: 36–40

Sackett DL, Rosenberg WMC, Muir Gray JA, Haynes RB, Richardson WS (1996) Evidence based medicine. What it is and what it isn't, *British Medical Journal* 312: 71–2

Sandelowski M and Barroso J (2002) Reading qualitative studies, *International Journal of Qualitative Studies* 1(1)

Sandelowski M, Docherty S, Emden C (1997) Qualitative metasynthesis. Issues and techniques, *Research in Nursing and Health* 20: 365–71

Skelton J and Edwards SLJ (2000) The function of the discussion section in academic medical writing, *British Medical Journal* 320: 1269–70

Tang H Hwee and Kwoon Ng J (2006) Googling for a diagnosis – use of Google as a diagnostic aid: internet based study, *British Medical Journal* 333: 1143–45

Thorne SE (2001) The implications of disciplinary agenda on quality criteria for qualitative research, in Morse J, Swanson JM, Kuzel AJ (eds) *The nature of qualitative evidence*. SAGE Publications: Thousand Oaks, California

Thorne SE, Jensen L, Kearney MH, Noblit G, Sandelowski M (2004) Qualitative metasynthesis. Reflections on methodological orientation and ideological agenda, *Qualitative Health Research* 14(10): 1342–65

Thouless RH and Thouless CR (1953) *Straight and Crooked Thinking* (4th edn). Hodder and Stoughton: Sevenoaks

Wakefield AJ, Murch SH, Anthony A, Linnell J (1998) Ileal-lymphoid-nodular hyperplasia, non-specific colitis and pervasive developmental disorder in children, *Lancet* 351: 637–41 (paper now withdrawn)

Watson, G (1987) *Writing a Thesis: a Guide to Long Essays and Dissertations*. London: Longman

Webb C (1992) The use of the first person in academic writing: objectivity, language and gatekeeping, *Journal of Advanced Nursing* 17: 747–52

Index

Related books from Open University Press
Purchase from www.openup.co.uk or order through your local bookseller

STUDY SKILLS FOR NURSING AND MIDWIFERY STUDENTS
Philip Scullion and David Guest

This book is an essential course companion for nursing and midwifery students at degree and diploma level, as well as those returning to study.

It covers key skills and knowledge needed, such as:

- Study strategies
- Reflective practice
- Critical thinking
- Evidence-based research
- Exam techniques
- Literature searching
- How to succeed in assessments

Lively and accessible, the book includes bullet points and exercises that will enhance reader efficiency in learning.

The book also has an accompanying website, www.openup.co.uk/nursing success, that is written specifically for this market, and includes tips on:

- Writing CVs and covering letters
- Finding a good job
- Interview skills
- Continuing professional development (CPD) for nurses and midwives
- Career progression

Study Skills for Nursing and Midwifery Students has been carefully structured to be used throughout a nursing career: It is key reading for new students in midwifery and all fields of nursing, as well as qualified staff who aim to enhance their professional development.

Contents
Series editor's preface – Part 1: The student nurse and midwife as a novice learner – Part 2: Beginning to develop effective study skills – Part 3: Becoming competent: Advanced learning for nursing and midwifery students – Part 4: Demonstrating proficiency through assessment – Part 5: Expertise for success: The lifelong learner in nursing and midwifery – References – Glossary – Index.

2007 192pp
ISBN-13: 978 0 335 22220 9   (ISBN-10: 0 335 22220 X) Paperback
ISBN-13: 978 0 335 22221 6   (ISBN-10: 0 335 22221 8) Hardback

THE COMPLETE GUIDE TO REFERENCING AND AVOIDING PLAGIARISM

Colin Neville

- Why is there so much emphasis on citing sources in some written work?
- How can I be sure I am referencing sources correctly?
- What is plagiarism and how do I avoid it?

There is a great deal of emphasis on accurate referencing in written work for university students, and those writing for professional purposes, but little information on the 'when', the 'why', as well as the 'how' of referencing. This book fills that gap, giving clear guidelines on how to correctly cite from external sources, what constitutes plagiarism, and how it can be avoided.

A unique feature of the book is the comparisons it makes between different referencing styles – such as Harvard, APA, MLA and Numerical referencing styles – which are shown side-by-side. This provides a useful guide, for students as they progress through higher education, and particularly for those on combined studies courses – who may be expected to use two, and sometimes three, different referencing styles.

Other special features in the book include:

- Essays demonstrating referencing in action
- Exercises on when to reference, and on what is, and what is not, plagiarism
- A 'Frequently Asked Questions' section on the referencing issues that most often puzzle people
- A detailed guide to referencing electronic sources, and advice on how to choose reliable Internet sites

A Complete Guide to Referencing and Avoiding Plagiarism is essential reading for all students and professionals who need to use referencing to accurately reflect the work of others and avoid plagiarism.

Contents
Preface – Acknowledgements – Referencing – Why reference? – What, when and how to reference – Plagiarism – Referencing styles – Harvard style of referencing – American Psychological Association (APA) and Modern Languages Association (MLA) referencing styles – Numerical referencing styles – Frequently asked questions – Referencing in action: example references – Index.

2007 240pp
ISBN-13: 978 0 335 22089 2   (ISBN-10: 0 335 22089 4) Paperback
ISBN-13: 978 0 335 22090 8   (ISBN-10: 0 335 22090 8) Hardback

SUCCESSFUL QUALITATIVE HEALTH RESEARCH
Emily Hansen

I strongly recommend this book to all those looking to undertake ethical and rigorous qualitative research in the field of health and health care.

Jon Adams, University of Newcastle, Australia and University of Leeds, UK

A practical overview for health students and health professionals embarking on an applied research project using a qualitative approach.

Successful Qualitative Health Research offers a thorough introduction to the field, written in a clear and concise fashion. Emphasising the rigorous approach required in health research, it provides a step-by-step guide to designing a research project using qualitative methods, and to collecting, analysing and presenting different types of data.

Hansen provides essential insights into the ideas and arguments underpinning different qualitative methods, and highlights the links between theory and practice. She also explains the importance of choosing the most appropriate form of data analysis. Each chapter features real life examples from experienced researchers from a wide range of health fields. These examples show how researchers have overcome common problems and offer inspiration and guidance.

Applied qualitative research is increasingly being used to explore a range of issues in health, both on its own and as an adjunct to quantitative research. This book offers a clear, no-nonsense approach that will be invaluable to students and professionals in nursing, medicine, allied health and public health.

Contents
Preface – Acknowledgements – Qualitative research: An introduction – Planning your research – Research design and rigour – Observation and participant observation – Interviewing – Focus groups – Analysing qualitative data – Writing qualitative research – Glossary – References – Index.

2006 240pp
ISBN-13: 978 0 335 22034 2   (ISBN-10: 0 335 22034 7) Paperback
ISBN-13: 978 0 335 22035 9   (ISBN-10: 0 335 22035 5) Hardback